KEN HEMPHILL
MIRROR, MIRROR ON THE WALL

Discovering Your True Self Through
SPIRITUAL GIFTS

BROADMAN PRESS
NASHVILLE, TENNESSEE

4210-37
ISBN: 0-8054-1037-6

Dewey Decimal Classification: 234.14
Subject Heading: GIFTS, SPIRITUAL
Library of Congress Card Catalog Number: 92-8
Printed in the United States of America

Unless otherwise noted, all Scripture quotations are from the *New American Standard Bible*. © The Lockman Foundation, 1960, 1962, 1963, 1968, 1971, 1972, 1973, 1975, 1977. Used by permission. Scripture quotations marked (KJV) are from the *King James Version*. Scripture quotations marked (NEB) are from the *New English Bible*. Copyright © The Delegates of the Oxford University Press and the Syndics of the Cambridge University Press, 1961, 1970. Reprinted by permission.

Library of Congress Cataloging-in-Publication Data

Hemphill, Kenneth S., 1948-
    Mirror, mirror on the wall : discovering your true self through
spiritual gifts / Ken Hemphill.
        p.   cm.
    Rev. ed. of: Spiritual gifts. 1988.
    ISBN 0-8054-1037-6
    1. Gifts, Spiritual.   I. Hemphill, Kenneth S., 1948-   . Spiritual
gifts.   II. Title.
BT767.3.H45   1992
234'.13—dc20   92-8
                                                               CIP

CONTENTS

To my first born daughter Kristina,
a truly gifted and lovely Christian lady.

On the joyous occasion
of your graduation.

With the prayer that you will
always employ your gifts
for the glory of God
and the enrichment of His church.

Preface

"Do you think God could ever love a person like *me*?" she asked, with the obvious emphasis on *me*. To this point in our conversation, she had not once dared to look up from the hole she was staring into the carpet in my office.

The fact that she was sitting before me was a minor miracle. Her first visit had taken weeks to arrange. An agonized letter had arrived in my office in response to a televised sermon. I had received numerous letters and cards from our viewers, but none like this. The pain, the loneliness, the broken spirit were so obvious in the hand written cry for help that I did not even need to read between the lines. The tone was such that I feared for her very life.

I immediately called her back and sent her a note of encouragement. She was overwhelmed to think that someone would actually care enough to respond to her cry. She apologized over and over again for taking my time. In a child-like manner she needed reassurance that she wasn't bothering me. Finally after weeks, she had plucked up the courage to make that agonizing first visit to my office.

When you find your true gifted identity in Christ, you will discover why you are here and how to please your Creator. This discovery brings a lasting and healthy self-image.

Her story, unfortunately, was an all too familiar one to many pastors, counselors, and friends of family. She had been rejected by her husband, "a religious giant," who had convinced her that she was unworthy of his love or anyone's for that matter. Her husband's message had been confirmed by a scare-tactic-sermon from a legalistic pastor, aimed at no one in particular, but deadly on target for this already-wounded lady who had been told by so many others that not even God could love her.

Sitting before me, head buried in hands, was an attractive, well-dressed lady in her mid-thirties. Why couldn't she look up? Why was she so depressed, so crushed? Why couldn't she accept God's love? Why was she so convinced she was worthless?

Her self-image had been completely crushed, and she had become absolutely paralyzed. It had affected her ability and desire to work, her functioning as a mother, and her ability to interact meaningfully with others.

Hers was a severe case, but wounded persons with low self-esteem are all around us and the number grows daily. Not only does it traumatize their own life, but it renders them incapable of making any meaningful impact for the Kingdom of God. After weeks of reassurance from God's Word concerning her worth to the Heavenly Father, we have seen the first signs of recovery. She now has a sense of hope.

What do we have to offer to overcome this paralyzing disease? The world offers many solutions, but few seem to give long term results and many have an unbiblical over-emphasis on *self*. There is a lasting and biblical solution. When you find your true gifted identity in Christ, you will discover why you are here and how to please your Creator. This discovery brings a lasting and healthy self-image.

This book has been a labor of love because I have received confirmation in the process by many with whom I have shared its contents. Special thanks are owed to my secretary Diane Styron who has the gift of administration which has enabled me to have additional time to work on this manuscript. Renee Daniel, one of our gifted singles, has contributed to the practical side of the manuscript.

This book is a testament to our gifted staff. I can see their influence on every page of this book. Larry White has helped me to understand the vital role of worship in building one's relationship with Christ. Steve O'Brien has helped my children to appreciate music and to see in it a way to express their faith. Tony Morris has gifts in the areas of audio and video that have challenged me to think about how these relate to the body of Christ. Wayne Jones has given invaluable suggestions on the self-image inventory and the practical dimensions of spiritual gifts, as well as capably leading our Sunday School. Doyle Chauncey has the gift of helps, and without him I would have been hopelessly lost on my computer. Gerry Peak is so creative he has constantly challenged my thinking. Dick Baker embodies the gift of helps and inspires me to be a servant. Pat Philbrick and Phyllis Cooke have built a foundation of faith in my children. Mike James has continued to build a superstructure of faith and has been a pastor to my older two girls. Gail Motley has gifts of administration and hospitality. She has facilitated many members in finding how to employ their gifts in the life of the church. For these gifted servants I will be always indebted.

I am always thankful to my wife Paula and my three daughters Kristina, Rachael, and Katie for the sacrifices they make for my writing ministry.

Mirror, Mirror

"Mirror, mirror on the wall, Who's the fairest of them all?" That classic line from the story of Snow White is still etched on my mind from childhood. The wicked queen repeated that question day after day with similar results. Things went well if the magic mirror told the queen what she wanted to hear, that she still reigned in beauty. If, perchance, another lady was named, the queen flew into a rage and had the usurper killed.

With the mirror's daily reassurance, the queen went about her affairs confident that she was worthy to reign. One day the queen's comfortable world was turned upside down when her trusty magic mirror replied: "Her lips blood red, her hair like night, Her skin like snow, her name—Snow White!" Another pretender for the queen's coveted role of "most beautiful"! Apparently Snow White had blossomed into a beauty, or the queen had passed her prime. The crow's feet at the corners of her eyes and the wrinkles on her forehead may have protruded through the everaccumulating layers of makeup. It is difficult to fool the mirror forever. Perhaps her liquid protein diet was losing ground to the cumulative effects of gravity. The queen was surely sagging.

Whatever the cause of this sudden reversal of fortunes, this word from the mirror ruined her day, and for that matter, the rest of her life. She became driven by the singular desire to destroy the new beauty in the land.

As a child I never quite understood why being second best to Snow White was so traumatic. Actually the runner-up position in a beauty contest is not all that bad. Bert Parks always informed us that if for any reason Miss America couldn't fulfill her duties the runner-up would step right in and assume her reign. Maybe the queen had watched those pageants, because she quickly devised a strategy to regain her favored position of number one beauty in the land. She summoned a huntsman and commissioned him to destroy her rival. The rest of her life, or at least of the story, is spent in the attempt to eliminate the beautiful princess and regain her identity as the fairest in the land.

You remember the rest of the story as the insanely jealous queen attempted to destroy the young beauty. No matter how many times we saw the movie or read the story we remained breathless to the end. Good prevailed and Snow White was awakened from her poisoned sleep by the charming prince on the white horse, and they lived happily ever after.

I wonder what happened to the queen. Did she live her life a bitter old woman? Did she lock herself away in the castle and refuse to face her public because she was no longer the fairest in the land? I know it's just a fairy tale, but how could a one-liner from a mirror on the wall ruin anyone's life?

A Poor Self-image

If we were to diagnose the queen's problem today we might say she had a poor self-image. Think about it for a minute. She must have been a beautiful woman. There is no reason to suspect that she and Snow White were the only two women who lived in the mythical kingdom. For years she had reigned supreme as the most beautiful woman in all the land. That should have counted for something. And remember she was the queen. There must have been certain perks that went with being queen, like power and money. Didn't those things count for something? Why couldn't she be happy being a wealthy queen who was the second most beautiful woman in the land? And why did this powerful woman require daily reassurance from her trusted mirror? And why did her world fall apart when she lost her coveted position as most beautiful?

We can only assume that her entire system of self-esteem was built on her physical beauty. When age, wrinkles, and assorted bulges wrested the title from her, life lost its meaning. Seems hard to believe, doesn't it, that a silly one-liner from a magic mirror could ruin one's life?

Yet the matter of self-image is not just the stuff of fairy tales. It is as real as we are. The self-image we carry does affect the way we function and cope with life itself. Some of us still carry one-liners from childhood mirrors that keep us paralyzed in our personal relationships and our ability to function meaningfully. One-liners like: "You'll never amount to anything;" "She's an ugly duckling;" "Where were you, kid, when the brains were handed out?" or "Sometimes I wish you had never been born." Invectives spoken in haste, often retracted with profuse apologies, but not before they found their mark and delivered their poisoned message, "You're no Snow White."

Repairing Our Self-image

Could the queen have been helped? Could she have lived happily ever after in spite of the fact that her beauty title had been taken away by Snow White? It appears to me that at least a part of her problem was basing her entire self-image in the constant affirmation of her physical beauty. When that faded, the rest of her accomplishments took on diminished value.

Just a fairy story?

All of us encounter individuals like this insecure queen. Their whole understanding of value and self-image has been wrongly placed and then unceremoniously shattered by a one-liner from some important mirror in their life. That talking mirror may be a parent, a spouse, or another significant person such as a coach, teacher, or pastor. In spite of all their virtues and accomplishments, all the accolades earned by constant striving, it is impossible for them to believe in themselves. They become discouraged, disillusioned, and paralyzed.

In fact, we are all impacted by the talking mirrors in our lives. Some of us are unsure and seek daily reaffirmation that we are "OK." When our mirror affirms us we go joyfully through the day, secure in our self-identity, but when the mirror fails to deliver the much-needed reassurance, our world crumbles.

How can we repair a distorted and debilitating self-image? Then once repaired, where can we find a reliable talking mirror that will provide constant healthy reaffirmation?

On an airplane the other day, I picked up a magazine which contained over thirty pages of tapes, videos, and books, many directed at the issue of self-esteem. Some focus on diet and exercise, others on self-discipline, and still others on visualization techniques. Many of these promise that you can achieve your goals by changing your self-image. Many are focused on the business person who has plateaued on the climb up the corporate ladder. Everyone seems to agree that our self-image needs a good overhaul. But how? All these answers can't be correct. Some seem to conflict with our scriptural convictions. Must we compromise our belief in God's Word to find our true self? Should we look inward, outward, or upward? It all seems so confusing and, at $89.95 for six tapes, who can afford to shop around for answers?

What are the elements upon which we build our self-identity and thus our sense of worth? Seven building blocks appear to be essential to a positive self-image.

- A sense of inherent worth.
- A knowledge that I am secure.
- A strong self-concept.
- A sense of purpose.
- An awareness that I belong.
- A sense of empowerment.
- A feeling of personal competence.

This book comes out of the conviction that the only way to repair a distorted self-image and to develop a healthy one is to be found in the Word of God. If we want to find a mirror that will truthfully and constructively affirm us, we must turn to our Creator, the one who created us out of His love, knows us intimately, and has a purpose for our being.

Some of us still carry one-liners from childhood mirrors that keep us paralyzed in our personal relationships and our ability to function meaningfully.

The Bible is full of image-enhancing statements. Who could imagine a love so great that the Sovereign God of the universe would give His only begotten Son that we might know Him and have everlasting life? Jesus declared that He had come that we might have life and that abundantly. Jesus continually taught His disciples about God's desire to give them His good gifts in abundance. If an earthly father knows how to give good gifts, then how much more will our Heavenly Father do? We are assured that nothing can separate us from the love of God in Christ Jesus. We are called His beloved, children of God, heirs and fellow heirs, the bride of Christ, and a people whom God desires to possess. Did you know you are being transformed daily into the image of Christ? You can reject the old one-liners that destroyed your self-esteem and hear God's affirmation.

Spiritual gifts are individualized endowments of grace from the Father, equipping you to play a vital role in His plan for the redemption of the world.

Yet in spite of all those assurances, many Bible-believing Christians remain unconvinced. Those promises seem like empty words and fancy phrases that work for someone else, but not you. You need something that gives you that firm assurance that you're worthwhile. What if I were to tell you that the Sovereign God of the universe created you with a purpose in mind and that He gifted you to accomplish that purpose and then placed you, individually, in His family just as He Himself chose? Notice that this knowledge would enable us to have an affirmative response to each of the seven building blocks of a strong self-image.

That is precisely what spiritual gifts are all about. Spiritual gifts are individualized endowments of grace from the Father, equipping you to play a vital role in His plan for the redemption of the world. Thus, discovering your unique giftedness is a first step toward a positive self-image. We can hear the assuring word of the Father, "Well done, good and faithful servant" (Matt. 25:23, KJV).

This book is about finding your gifts and putting them to work. We will begin first with God's love letter to us, the Bible. The first section of the book looks at some of the important passages about spiritual gifts. Many believers have ignored some of these passages because they have been misinterpreted or misused in an arrogant and sometimes hurtful way. Our study should remove the fog of confusion and pave the way for a healthy and productive understanding of spiritual gifts. The last two chapters lead you through the steps to discovering your gift(s) and your unique place in the body of Christ.

At the end of this chapter, you'll find a simple self-image inventory. Take a few moments to complete this activity before you continue.

The Book of James compares the Word of God to a mirror which honestly reflects our true selves. "But one who looks intently at the perfect law, the law of liberty, and abides by it, not having become a forgetful hearer but an effectual doer, this man shall be blessed in what he does" (1:25). I believe that the discovery that awaits in the pages of this book could liberate you from the false mirrors of the past and provide a reliable mirror of daily affirmation. You are of worth; your Creator made you so.

Self-image Scale

Directions:
Circle the number that most represents
your present feelings about yourself
1 = Never   5 = Always

1. I feel good about myself.	1	2	3	4	5
2. I feel secure.	1	2	3	4	5
3. I feel I know myself well.	1	2	3	4	5
4. I know what I want out of life.	1	2	3	4	5
5. I am accepted by others.	1	2	3	4	5
6. I feel able to handle my situation.	1	2	3	4	5
7. I am confident in my ability to perform.	1	2	3	4	5
8. I base my feelings about myself on my worth, not my performance.	1	2	3	4	5
9. I have a sense of peace even in the midst of adversity.	1	2	3	4	5
10. I like who I am.	1	2	3	4	5
11. My commitments are based on my priorities.	1	2	3	4	5
12. I feel that I am welcome in my social groups.	1	2	3	4	5
13. I feel like I have control of my destiny.	1	2	3	4	5
14. I feel that I can accomplish anything I set my mind to do.	1	2	3	4	5
15. I feel good about myself even when I have made mistakes in my life.	1	2	3	4	5
16. I know that no matter what happens I will be OK.	1	2	3	4	5

17. I understand who I am.   1   2   3   4   5

18. I have specific goals for my life and evaluate them on an ongoing basis.   1   2   3   4   5

19. I feel that I am accepted for who I am, not what I do.   1   2   3   4   5

20. I have the ability to accomplish great things.   1   2   3   4   5

21. I am knowledgeable and competent in my work.   1   2   3   4   5

Scoring

Place the appropriate value for each answer in the appropriate box below. When you have completed each box, total across. After completing each total box add down to get your grand total score.

				Total	
Inherent Worth	1 ___	8 ___	15 ___	___	*If you scored:*
Sense of Security	2 ___	9 ___	16 ___	___	15-13 = Excellent
Self-Concept	3 ___	10 ___	17 ___	___	12-10 = Good
Sense of Purpose	4 ___	11 ___	18 ___	___	9- 7 = Fair
Sense of Belonging	5 ___	12 ___	19 ___	___	6- = Poor
Sense of Empower-ment	6 ___	13 ___	20 ___	___	
Feeling of Personal Competence	7 ___	14 ___	21 ___	___	

Grand Total _____

Self-image

Total Self-image Score

If your Grand Total score was

     85-105   —Your self-image is *excellent*
     57- 84   —Your self-image is *good*
     43- 56   —Your self-image is *average*
     22- 42   —Your self-image is *fair*
     21-Below—Your self-image is *poor*

Looking in the Mirror

How do we begin this search for our true identity and healthy self-image? You may be thinking, *I've tried so many different avenues that haven't helped I don't know where to begin. My subliminal tapes apparently didn't connect, the diet that made my friends look like starlets just made me hungry, dressing for success only wiped out my already suffering bank account, and my positive thinking course made me even more positive that I would always be a failure.* Many of the tapes and books designed to help you discover your true identity and develop a healthy self-image have one common flaw. They begin with the individual. They focus on the person and say little about the community in which that person lives. Many of these image-building books and tapes are self-centered and actually compound the problems of the person struggling with a poor self-image.

These popular books urge us to pull ourselves up by our own bootstraps, to look out for number one, to visualize what we want to be. We can ascend the corporate ladder, achieve wealth and success, and project ourselves into new levels of competence. I'm sure that many of these self-help gurus are well-meaning, but the advice they are giving has proved in many instances to be destructive to personal relationships and ultimately to self-image.

In the guise of image building, I have seen men and women neglect their families to look out for number one. For a while they seem to have it all together. They walk with a new swagger, talk with a new bravado, and their new image propels them on their way to much-wanted success. Yet the path is more barren than they imagined as they isolate themselves from their true friends and colleagues. The costs begin to mount as they discover that their own children see them as distant strangers, and finally their marriage relationship cools from neglect. Some have actually left their families "to find themselves." Single adults bent on looking out for number one at any

16

cost frequently find the risk far greater than the reward. They may find business success, but their ruthless aggression isolates them from the thing they desired most—to be loved and accepted. Their self-esteem takes another lick.

Any time we put self first, we become demanding and rebellious. Our priority concern becomes "getting my way." Must we go to such extreme ends and risk so much to discover our true self-worth? For the Christian we must ask several other questions about this obsessive emphasis on *self*. Does it square with the Bible's focus on discovering greatness through service and sacrifice? And what about the admonition to "be subject to one another in the fear of Christ" (Eph. 5:21)? No! It doesn't! And we must! Those are the answers to the three questions just posed.

Can we then discover a path to a healthy self-image that doesn't alienate us in our relationships and is biblical in its emphasis? Yes we can. Remember, we are taught that we must love our neighbor as ourselves. If we don't love ourselves we will have little ability to love another. But if our love of self does not lead us to love our neighbor then it becomes self-centered and destructive.

The Bible presents a better solution to developing a healthy self-image. It is a solution that is not self-focused, but community oriented. It is not self-actualizing, but divinely empowered. It is not achieved by positive thinking, but by appropriating God's perfect promises and discovering His gracious gifts.

What Is the Scene?

We begin our journey in Thessalonica, the largest and most important city in Macedonia. This seaport city was a wealthy and flourishing center of trade. It is not surprising that the apostle Paul wanted to plant a church in this pivotal city. According to Luke's account, Paul began his ministry in Thessalonica by teaching the residents in the local synagogue for three Sabbaths (Acts 17:1-10). The scene in Acts abruptly shifts to a citywide uproar that resulted in the harassment of Jason and the brethren and the quick departure of Paul. While Acts only mentions the three weeks of Paul's ministry in the synagogue, it is likely that his ministry in Thessalonica was considerably longer.

If we look at Paul's pattern for ministry in other communities we can gain some insight into what probably happened in Thessalonica.

In Corinth, for example, Paul began his ministry by reasoning in the synagogue every Sabbath. As the resistance arose among the Jews, he left the synagogue and continued his ministry in the home of Titus Justus (Acts 18:4-7).

Paul did the same thing at Ephesus. He entered the synagogue and spoke boldly for three months. Again, opposition arose as his message that Jesus was the fulfillment of Jewish prophecies concerning the Messiah hit home. Paul withdrew with his followers and continued to teach in the school of Tyrannus (Acts 19:8-9).

Paul probably continued his ministry in Thessalonica from the home of Jason after his preaching in the synagogue caused such an uproar. The controversy over Paul's preaching was fanned into white-hot flame after a number of Jews and God-fearing Greeks responded to Paul's message and joined Paul and Silas. Truly this man was turning their world upside down! To rid the city of this menace, the Jews sought the help of the thugs in the marketplace and turned the city into a cauldron of unrest.

Can we then discover a path to a healthy self-image that doesn't alienate us in our relationships and is biblical in its emphasis?

Knowing that Paul would be teaching at Jason's home, the lynch mob rushed to his residence. Paul, however, was gone, having been secreted out of town by Jason and some of the brethren. The mob, angry for revenge, dragged Jason and some of the brethren before the authorities. Angrily, they shouted: "These men who have upset the world have come here also; and Jason has welcomed them, and they all act contrary to the decrees of Caesar, saying that there is another king, Jesus" (Acts 17:7). The Jews knew that the civil authorities would be uninterested in a religious dispute so they couched their charges in such a way that Paul's preaching sounded like treason.

There is a striking similarity between the accusation hurled at these early Christians and those which were used to bring Jesus to crucifixion. The word translated *Christ* in the Greek is the Hebrew equivalent of "Messiah" which meant "The Anointed One." This term was used throughout the Old Testament to refer to the king of Israel. The Christian confession that Jesus was the Messiah could easily be distorted to accuse them of subversive activities "saying that there is another king, Jesus."

The city authorities heard the accusations but could do little since the troublemakers, Paul and Silas, were nowhere to be found. Jason and the others were released after the authorities received a pledge or bond from them assuring the authorities that there would be no repetition of the trouble. While the city authorities may have considered the matter closed, some of the townspeople did not. The hostility that led to Paul's quick departure continued even after Paul was gone.

In order to destroy the struggling young community, the detractors mounted a slander campaign against Paul and his work in Thessalonica. When you read Paul's impassioned self-defense in 1 Thessalonians 1—3 you will see that their attack had met with some measure of success. Paul expressed his anxiety for the welfare of the Thessalonian Christians and also for their relationship to him (3:6). You might wonder how such trumped-up charges against the apostle could have met with success. Surely, you would think, they could have seen through these flimsy charges.

The one clue that helps us to understand this matter is Paul's hasty and secretive departure. Given the volatile circumstances, it appears that "Jason and some brethren," a small inner circle of leaders, had been responsible for secreting Paul and Silas out of town. Many of the Thessalonican believers were not personally aware of the details of Paul's departure. They simply knew that they were suffering from the hostility aimed at Paul and he was conspicuously absent.

Put yourself in their place. How would you feel if the man in whom you had placed great confidence suddenly left the church during a very difficult period? Now add to your loss the fact that you are bearing the brunt of the harassment that had been prompted by this man's ministry.

Paul's sudden disappearance and his failure to return provided his detractors with a golden opportunity to attack the young Christian community. If they could raise doubts about the integrity of the apostle, they could call into question his teaching and the very existence of the church itself. Fleeing the scene could imply guilt. Discrediting a teacher or preacher by personal attack upon his or her character and motive continues even in our day. Many young Christians have been severely wounded when their pastor came under attack or suffered a personal moral failure. Sometimes the message is rejected along with the messenger.

This could explain why Paul devoted much of the first three chapters of 1 Thessalonians to a defense of his tactics, behavior, message, and results while in Thessalonica. He assured his readers that his message did not spring from "error or impurity or by way of deceit" (2:3). He certainly could not be accused of greed since he had worked night and day to support himself (vv. 5-9).

Paul wanted the community at Thessalonica to continue on in the faith and therefore soon after his hasty departure, he sent Timothy to strengthen and encourage the believers (3:2). Timothy returned to Paul with a largely positive report, but with the news that there was ongoing persecution and some tension in the community itself. Timothy also informed Paul about several matters of confusion that existed about his teaching.

Thus Paul wrote this letter for several apparent reasons. He felt he needed to vindicate himself fully for the sake of the community. Second, Paul wanted to assure their continued growth by the building up of their faith (v. 10). Since circumstances in Thessalonica prevented his return, he sent a personal letter to remind them of his teaching and to clarify any points of confusion. Third, and most important, he wanted to provide for the ongoing life of the community by providing specific instructions concerning community ministry. Paul was well aware that the future of Christianity in Thessalonica depended upon the ability of the body of believers to encourage and minister to one another.

One of the recurring themes of the entire teaching section which begins in chapter four is the maintaining of proper relationships in the community. For example, when addressing sexual purity, Paul cautioned them: "that no man transgress and defraud his brother" (v. 6). Paul exhorted them to continue to improve brotherly love. The entire discussion of the second coming of the Lord is focused by the exhortation: "comfort one another with these words" (v. 18; cf. 5:11). All the problems faced by this community could best be met by the mutual encouragement one of another and by the loving recognition of those who have charge over them in the Lord.

When we deal with spiritual matters, particularly highly individualistic ones such as spiritual gifts and the discovery of our self-image, we tend to focus exclusively on ourselves. This often leads to the same introverted and selfish emphasis of many of the world's approaches to self-image. The discovery of and use of our gifts must be anchored in the context of community. God gives the spiritual gifts with the good of the community in view, and therefore if we are to discover our authentic God-given image, we must remain biblically and practically anchored to the fellowship of the body of Christ through the local church.

What Is the Problem?

Whenever I do conferences on church growth or spiritual gifts, I hear horror stories about internal struggles over power and authority. Sometimes it involves the pastor and deacons or elders, and in other instances it involves various members of the church. Whatever the case, the results are stunted church growth and inactivity on the part of many church members. The attitude seems to be; "I'll let these folks hash it out, I've got better things to do with my time." We must deal with this sort of problem for the sake of the ministry of the church and the discovery of personal worth of every single member.

Paul's first remarks in our community ministry passage have to do with proper relationships between the brethren and those in leadership positions. The fact that Paul had twice just encouraged all the Christians in Thessalonica to encourage and build one another up did not alter the fact that some members had been gifted to be community leaders. A spiritually gifted body and pastoral leadership are not conflicting but complementary concepts.

The discovery of and use of our gifts must be anchored in the context of community.

The phrase "diligently labor" (5:12) underlines the magnitude of the intense physical exertion required of the community leaders. Furthermore Paul probably used this particular phrase to describe the persons who were to be esteemed as leaders. When you read 1 and 2 Thessalonians you will notice that some individuals wanted to be community leaders, but they were not willing to work, even to support their own families. These men had become a disturbance to the community, and their presence had created confusion and difficulty for the authentic leaders. We often find a good number of church members who are willing to volunteer for positions of leadership for the honor and prestige it bestows. They are often less excited about the heavy commitment of work required to accomplish the task.

Paul called the members causing the internal dissension in Thessalonica the "unruly" (v. 14), a military term that means to stand out of rank. The discussion in 2 Thessalonians 3:7-11 suggests their refusal to work was a central element of their unruly behavior. These men had disobeyed Paul's teaching and had spread dissent in the community by behaving like busybodies. The cartoon character, Lucy, in the "Peanuts" comic strip well illustrates this nagging, destructive personality type. Unruly persons polarize people and destroy the unity of the fellowship. They seek to lead by intimidation, and they actually keep many members from discovering their unique ministry and gifts within the community.

Paul's first concern was thus to identify and undergird the true leaders of the church so that there could be peace and unity. Such an atmosphere will provide for the proper context for gift discovery and mutual ministry.

Paul's Instructions

The Functions of Leaders

What is the role of leaders in the life of the church? How does their gifted ministry enable other members of the body to discover and develop their gifts? In 1 Thessalonians 5:12-13 we discover several clues concerning the proper relationship of gifted leader and gifted member.

Certain individuals in Thessalonica needed the brethren's recognition and love for the successful completion of their ministry, which would in turn result in the strengthening of the whole community. Paul insisted that they deserved recognition and esteem because of their work. The mission of the church is so critical that proper relationships among the many members stands as a high priority. Paul used the terms "labor among you," "have charge over you," and "give you instruction" (v. 12) to describe the scope of the ministry of the church leaders.

The term "labor" conveys the idea of hard work. To labor among also suggests the pastoral function of the leader who works alongside his flock. He leads by example and encouragement. He nurtures the flock and enables them to serve in their God-given capacities.

One of the primary functions of the pastoral leader is that of leading, protecting, or managing. In 1 Timothy 3:4-5 we read a similar description of the administrative work of pastoral leaders. In that context the management function in the church is compared to the similar function of the father as the head of the home. Thus the primary task being described is that of leading or administrating in the life of the church. The church without a clearly identified leader is likely to go off in all directions at once and then confusion reigns. It is essential that the church have strong pastoral leadership in order to enable all the individual members to be empowered to fulfull their God-given tasks. The pastor's leadership is to reflect the patient and loving concern of the father whose desire it is to see to the total development of his children.

Leading certainly includes the idea of caring for and thus both senses of the word are probably in view here. Any leader, pastor, or otherwise, would do well to remember that authority to lead is tied to one's care for those being led. The phrase "in the Lord" places a boundary on the leader's authority. Leadership takes place by the calling of the Lord and only in the realm of spiritual affairs.

In recent years we have seen a healthy and biblical emphasis on the shared ministry of clergy and laity. The biblical understanding of spiritual gifts will offer greater encouragement to all of us in fulfilling our role in ministry. Yet we must not allow the discovery of shared ministry to cause us to depreciate the work of those called out by God for leadership roles in the church. Like parents in the healthy family they are called to lead by example, to oversee and give instruction. Such instruction will require warning and correction. These too must be accepted and acted upon to develop a healthy church with God-affirmed members.

We must renew our commitment to the biblical pattern for the church. The church must allow the pastoral leader to provide the visionary leadership which gives direction to its ministry. The church cannot treat the pastor as a hireling who is given little say in the direction of its ministry, or we will flounder without any clear direction or strategy. In the same manner, pastors must not attempt to exert authority in a strong-handed manner. They must earn it by laboring among and caring for the flock. Too much is at stake in the mission of the church to allow dysfunctional relationships to hamper the work of the church. Notice that the result of healthy relationships is the ability to "Live in peace with one another." This phrase from 1 Thessalonians 5:13 is the unifying theme of this whole letter. Paul's overarching desire was to establish harmonious relationships within the community so that the individual members could encourage one another in the face of persecution and the community could command the respect of the outsiders (4:12). The atmosphere of peace alone provides the platform that the members of the church, including the leaders, can accomplish their work unhindered.

The final term used to describe the work of the leader suggests a teaching function. It includes the idea of warning and correction. The pastor, as teacher, seeks to influence the mind and disposition of the church family by appropriate biblical instruction, wise counsel, warning, and correction. We don't like words like warning and correction, but they are essential to healthy church relationships as they are to healthy family relationships. Warning and correction direct people away from destructive behavior and toward personal growth.

Many churches and pastors have ignored this function because it can sometimes be difficult and unpleasant. It reminds me of my dad's favorite line just before he punished me: "Son this hurts me more than it does you." I had trouble believing that as a child, but now that I am a parent, I know it to be true. Confrontation with the purpose of bringing constructive warning and correction may be painful, but it may also be necessary to enable the church family to grow into full maturity and the individual members to discover their giftedness. If we look at the example of the apostle Paul, found in his letters, we will see that he frequently had to bring correction for the maturing of the church. Yet Paul administered correction in love and for the good of the church.

Recently I became distraught over the number of families in our church who were seriously contemplating divorce. Many were already separated and their friends were grieved by their apparent inability to reconcile their differences. I regularly teach on issues such as divorce and its consequences, but my pulpit admonitions were having few obvious results. The Lord convicted me concerning my personal inactivity to bring warning and correction. I knew that as pastor I should intervene, but I reasoned that they knew what I thought because of my preaching. The truth was that I find such situations awkward and I usually avoid personal confrontation.

I decided that I must make an attempt to bring warning and correction before it was too late. I wrote personal letters telling of my pastoral affection for both members of the marriage and of my desire to meet with them for prayer. To my surprise, some couples immediately responded and came to my office. In that meeting I warned them of the biblical and personal consequences of divorce. I pointed them to others in our church who had divorced and were now grieved by the residual consequences. I literally pleaded with them to reconsider and offered our full assistance at reconciliation. We then prayed together for an extended period. I have been involved in this project for some time and to date I have no sudden reversals to report, but I know such loving confrontation is essential to healthy family relationships.

The first couple who came affirmed me for my care. The wife commented that she wondered why someone had not approached them sooner with correction. Good question! If the church is going to be a healthy family, then warning and correction will be a balanced part of its total ministry, administered personally and in love by a pastor or fellow member who cares. Our deacons and care leaders through the Sunday School often have the opportunity to lovingly confront fellow-members in order to bring healing. The goal must always be healing and restoration, and we must be willing to invest time and energy to assist in the healing and growth process. Because we are family, we must love one another in word and deed. This will require time and energy, but it will pay rich dividends in the building of a healthy family as the context for the individual to discover their own self-identity.

We might call the leader described here the pastor, priest, parson, or vicar. Official titles did not seem to concern the first-century church as much as they do the twentieth-century church. An individual can claim whatever title he likes, but if the biblical functions of pastoral leadership are not being accomplished, the title has little meaning. Paul focused on gifted function rather than title. The leader must labor among, provide leadership, and give instruction. These three functions are still central to the work of the pastor and to the maturity of the church family for the individual discovery of gifts and meaningful ministry.

The Relationships of Family

The church is like a family and if the church family becomes dysfunctional then its work is hampered and its members are wounded. The proper context for discovering and utilizing one's giftedness is the community of fellowship we call the church. If we are going to unearth our biblical self-image, a healthy family is a necessity. We must therefore give high priority to developing proper relationships in our church family so that our mission is unhindered and the individual members are affirmed in their unique giftedness.

It is not surprising that Paul framed the discussion of community ministry with a call to loving relationships. Paul exhorted the Thessalonians to "appreciate" and "esteem highly in love" those who labored among them in a leadership position. No doubt, Paul's hasty departure created some tension. It may have not been entirely clear who was in charge. Some may have grown weary by what appeared to be power struggles between Jason and other brethren and those unruly members who were keeping the community stirred up. Paul appealed for loving relationships in the community because of the significance of the mission of the church. We are the bride of Christ, called and commissioned by God to fulfill the Great Commission. The church deals with eternal issues! For this reason, we must not allow anything to stand in the way of the proper functioning of the body.

Paul focused on gifted function rather than title.

I have often commented that I am not all of my people's favorite pastor. For some I will never replace a beloved former pastor. Often these deep loyalties were created by a bond forged during a critical and teachable moment. The "favorite pastor" may be the pastor who helped nurture a family through tragedy or who was there when their firstborn child came into the world. His ministry and impact left an indelible impression and he will forever be their pastor. Hey, that's OK! I don't have to be everyone's favorite pastor for our church to function properly. Yet I do need the love and respect of our people because of the significance of our work together. You may be the teacher of a Sunday School class that was taught for twenty years by a beloved teacher. You don't need to be defensive. You don't have to compete for affection. You only need to forge healthy relationships for the sake of the mutual goals of the class.

Our priority must be to develop and nurture loving relationships among all the people of the church including those in authority positions. We do this, not as a popularity contest, but because God commands it and our work together requires it.

Over the years I have seen the work of many fine churches in our community hampered because they lacked healthy interpersonal relationships. Every community has a church where there has been a constant parade of preachers. None of them stay very long. They all leave for different stated reasons. One preaches too long, another too short. One is too authoritative, the next is unwilling to lead. This parade of pastors not only affects the witness of that church, but it impacts the spiritual self-identity of the individual members. This same church often has staggered through numerous church splits as factions have sided with one leader over another.

Individual members who have been hurt by bickering and disputes often move to another church hoping to solve the problem. Many of these transfer members are reluctant to get involved and use their God-given abilities in their new church family. Their self-esteem has been wounded and thus their gifts lie unused. They don't want to get burned again. This is a double tragedy. It impacts the ministry of the church, and it destroys the self-esteem of the individual.

The church is like a family and if the church family becomes dysfunctional then its work is hampered and its members are wounded.

Thus the first step in gift discovery for the Christian is the identification with a local church where healthy family relationships can be developed. In a healthy church family, you will receive teaching by example as well as verbal instruction. Children in the home see examples as well as hear instruction. The gift discovery process requires both instruction and example. Working together in mutually caring relationships will often provide the positive affirmation you need to aid you in discovering your gifted purpose in the body. Accept the warning and correction, when necessary, as loving reproof enabling you to develop a healthy personal identity. The more the church family provides the context for positive instruction and feedback, the less will be the demand for corrective teaching.

The Shared Ministry

In verse 14 Paul repeated the term "brethren" to draw attention to the responsibilities for ministry shared by everyone in the community. The ministries here were tailored to the specific needs in Thessalonica. The "unruly" were in special need of warning and correction. They must be brought back into line for the good of the community. The "disconsolate" may be a reference to members distressed by the delay of the coming of the Lord or by the death of a friend. It could also refer to persons depressed by the present afflictions caused by the persecution of church. These individuals need to be consoled and encouraged.

The "weak" were members whose faith was shaky. They must be clung to! It is easy to allow the weak to slip through the cracks of our church fellowship. They are often too frail or hurting to ask for help. They drop out of church activities and isolate themselves. We sometimes give the impression that these weak folks should just "suck it up" and get on with life. In Galatians 6:1-2 Paul gave good advice on restoring those who have slipped because of personal weakness. They must be restored with a spirit of gentleness with the awareness that we may be the next to require restoration. In so doing we; "Bear one another's burdens and thus fulfill the law of Christ" (v. 2).

Verse 14 ends with the command to show patience to everyone. Patience has value for the unity of the ministering community. As our study unfolds you will see a demand for patience each time we study a community ministry passage. To work together in family relationships requires patience. The church member who feels the urge to criticize every program of the church, the single adult who feels his needs aren't being met, the child who demands constant attention, all call for patience from the ministering community. Too often we expect uniformity of spiritual growth from our members. The church, by its very nature, will always be made up of persons at different levels of spiritual maturity.

Further Paul exhorted them to "See that on one repays another with evil for evil, but always seek after that which is good for one another and for all men" (v. 15). You've seen the popular bumper sticker: "Don't get mad, get even." Tragically this attitude can rear its ugly head in the church. Paul not only prohibited getting even, he demanded they seek the good for one another. Redemptive behavior requires that we take the initiative to minister to those who do evil to us.

A child once wrote a letter to God, saying, "Did you really mean do unto others as they do unto you, because if you did then I'm going to fix my brother."[1] Misinterpretations such as this, coupled with basic human nature often brings out the "I'm going to fix my brother'' attitude in us. It takes a humble and patient spirit to seek reconciliation.

The leaders may be called to provide for caring, teaching, and administrating, but all the members of the church are called by God to build up the fellowship of the church by ministering to one another. Many of the duties that we have often assigned to the pastor are commanded of all the brethren. Have you ever found yourself thinking, *People keep dropping out of church. I wonder what's wrong? The pastor ought to be doing more to encourage these new members.* Could it be that God is calling you to do that?

The phrases in verses 16-21 relate to the gathered worship of the community. The participation in gathered worship is essential to the ongoing life of the community. Paul exhorted them to rejoice always, even in adversity, to pray unceasingly, and to give thanks. The source of divine power is tapped as the community gathers for worship. At the same time the community is knit together and built up from within.

It is refreshing to see that many churches are rediscovering the strength derived from effective worship. We should never allow worship to degenerate into a repetitive and dull ritual which is tolerated weekly. We must come prepared to encounter the living God. All of us need to participate regularly in worship. Our participation involves not just attendance, but singing, praying, giving, listening, bearing witness, and responding.

I have often noticed that many persons with servant spirits will volunteer to work during worship in the preschool. If these faithful volunteers are allowed to serve continuously without opportunity for worship, they will burn out and be lost to the fellowship. The caring church cannot permit this to happen. Perhaps you should offer to serve in the preschool one Sunday a month in order to allow a fellow member to participate in worship. Without worship we will not be refreshed by the Lord for service.

Finally Paul instructed the Thessalonians not to quench the work of the Spirit by despising prophetic utterances. We must be careful not to interpret this passage with the problems of 1 Corinthians 12— 14 in mind. Here Paul was not concerned with all the spiritual gifts, but only with prophecy. Prophecy refers to an intelligible message given under inspiration, whose content is from the Lord.

To despise prophetic utterance would quench the work of the Spirit. There were apparently various "prophetic voices" in Thessalonica. Not all of them were genuine, as 2 Thessalonians 2:2 demonstrates. Thus they could not accept all prophetic voices as genuine. They must "examine everything carefully" (v. 21). They must test the source and nature of the inspired utterances. Did they come from individuals who had proved themselves to be faithful servants of the Lord through their hard work on behalf of the community? Was the content consistent with sound teaching? Plenty of folks readily volunteer their prophetic wisdom about how to cure the ills of the church. To determine the validity of their message you should not only ensure that it is consistent with Scripture, but you should also look at the personal track record of the prophet. Does this individual serve in the community to bring about necessary changes for the good of the body?

Many of the duties that we have often assigned to the pastor are commanded of all the brethren.

Today anytime there is a scandal involving a pastor or television evangelist, there are individuals who want to lump all preachers together and ignore their teaching. We can readily see who wrong this would be and how detrimental it would be to the growth and unity of the community. Here, again, Paul seems to be encouraging the Thessalonians to heed the teaching of those how were truly God appointed leaders in their community.

Reflections in the Mirror

1. God calls certain persons in the community to function in leadership positions. They must labor among, provide leadership and instruction. Who are some of the persons in your church family who accomplish these functions? _____

2. The recognition and acceptance of these persons by the community assures the success of their ministry and builds the unity of the family and the general well-being of the community. If the community does not esteem their leaders in love, no amount of presumed authority will make their ministry effective. What can you do to recognize and encourage those who serve in leadership functions?

3. It is anticipated that every member will be involved in the ministry of building up the church. Unity and peace will be the result of every member ministry. Where do you think you fit in your church family? _____ Do you already serve in some ministry? What? _____ What would you like to do?

_____

4. This passage pays particular attention to personal relationships in the church. A healthy church family is a crucial factor in the enabling of the individual believer to discover and utilize his or her gifts. Identification with and participation in a healthy church family is the first critical step toward the discovery of one's gifted self-identity. Do you remember the seven foundational elements for healthy self-esteem? One involved the sense of belonging. If you do not have an active church home, that should be a first priority as you continue to read this book. Look for a church where the Bible is taught and healthy relationships exist among the members.

Note

1. Stuart Hample and Eric Marshall, *Children's Letters to God* (New York: Workman Publishing, 1991).

Distorted Images

Did you ever visit a fun house at the county fair when you were a child? My favorite was the House of Mirrors. My first visit was frightening, as it is for most children. It was quite a shock to see my reflection distorted in such a manner that it was barely recognizable. Then as I peered from mirror to mirror I understood why the distortion was taking place. The mirrors were bowed and skewered in various ways to present a sometimes humorous, but always distorted view.

Even as children, we didn't want to stand for long before a mirror that made us look about two feet high and three feet wide. Didn't do much for our self-image, I guess. I enjoyed standing in front of the elongated mirror which made me look to be about ten feet high. You could just imagine yourself slam-dunking over Bill Russell. This was, of course, before the days of Michael Jordan. Some of the mirrors created more exotic and multiple images of your body, but all alike were distortions. You could take comfort in the knowledge that once you left the fun house you would return "to plain, but normal you."

It's not quite that easy with the issue of self-image. It seems that once we've stood before a distorted mirror, the image stays ingrained in the hidden recesses of the mind and continues to affect our understanding of ourselves through much of our lives. That distorted mirror may have been a parent who made us feel two feet tall and shrinking. Unkind one-liners like: "You'll never amount to anything!; Why couldn't you be like your brother?; and "You're stupid!" can leave an indelible impression. This image from our childhood can hold us in bondage and keep us from achieving what God intended for us to be.

I have a really gifted friend who has many accomplishments of which he can be justifiably proud. He was an outstanding athlete in high school. He had his choice of colleges and a full scholarship to boot. As an adult he has done well in his business and is well liked by his peers at his church. Nevertheless, he still struggles with a poor self-image and his personal sense of worth because he has never felt that he measured up to his father's expectations. He was never good enough! This has led to a tragic results and futile attempts to get his aging father's attention and approval. He was never able to shed the distorted image indelibly imprinted by his childhood experiences. Before we can build a positive self-image, we must uncover and dispose of distorted images.

Our particular focus in this book is on the unearthing of our true self-image through the discovery and actualization of our God-given gifts and talents. If our Creator/Father offers His daily affirmation by uniquely gifting us for service in His family, then we have a solid foundation for an authentic and lasting self-image. But we must first throw out a caution sign. Mistaken claims about spiritual gifts can give a distorted view. An overexaggerated claim about their significance is like that elongated mirror that could make a young boy think he could slam-dunk one on Bill Russell. On the other side of the coin are people who believe themselves to be giftless. Their plight is like standing before the mirror that makes a reflection only two feet tall. Both are distorted images which must be rejected.

Once we've stood before a distorted mirror, the image stays ingrained in the hidden recesses of the mind.

In the next four chapters we will be looking at the church at Corinth because most of the biblical material on spiritual gifts is in 1 Corinthians. First, a little background on the church might prove to be helpful. This church was anything but boring!

The church at Corinth was well-known in the community; after all, some of the members of the church were battling it out in court. It seems that several of the members insisted on their rights, whether it was the freedom to dine in a pagan temple or for women to speak in the assembly with their heads uncovered. The entire community was talking about the last time the church celebrated the Lord's Supper. Some left hungry while the wealthier members were a bit tipsy from too much good wine. The church was scandalized by the word that a man was sleeping with his stepmother. Not everyone was upset by this last bit of news; some were even boasting that such behavior was proof of their advanced spirituality. The church was, in fact, divided on a lot of issues. Some claimed Paul, others Apollos or Cephas, while some simply argued they were for Christ.

The whole community was confused about the matter of spiritual gifts. Some claimed to speak with the tongues of angels. These folks saw their abundance of spiritual gifts as proof that they were spiritually advanced. In their own eyes they stood ten feet tall. This had caused others to see themselves as second-class citizens since they didn't possess these spectacular gifts. In fact, some of the spirituals had implied as much.

If our Creator/Father offers His daily affirmation by uniquely gifting us for service in His family, then we have a solid foundation for an authentic and lasting self-image.

Fortunately, the two Corinthian letters provide us with an abundance of material with which to build a reasonably accurate picture of the church at Corinth. Paul arrived in Corinth on the heels of several difficult ministry ventures. At Philippi, Thessalonica, and Berea he had a promising beginning that was cut short by fanatical Jews. In Athens he experienced little success. No wonder that, in his own words, he came "in weakness and in fear and in much trembling" (1 Cor. 2:3). Paul ministered in Corinth for eighteen months. He lodged with Aquila and Priscilla, Jewish Christians who had been expelled from Rome. He began his ministry in the synagogue, but soon moved to the house of Justus, next door to the synagogue, and continued his ministry from that location (Acts 18:1-17).

Paul's early converts in Corinth were Jews and devout pagans, who had become dissatisfied with pagan life and had attached themselves to the synagogue. These people are called "God-fearers" in the Bible and were often very receptive to the gospel.

After Paul departed Corinth, the local work was carried on by Stephanas, Fortunatus, and Achaicus (1 Cor. 16:17). Other leaders had visited Corinth, some like Apollos augmented Paul's message, while others seem to have created considerable confusion, particularly in regard to spiritual gifts. Some time after his departure Paul wrote a first letter to the Corinthians. The evidence for its existence is found in 1 Corinthians 5:9, but the letter itself perished. Its contents were misunderstood and thus the letter we call 1 Corinthians replaced that letter and there was no need for God to preserve it.

Members of the Corinthian church kept Paul abreast of the news. The household of Chloe, a wealthy merchant, brought Paul disheartening news that divisions had occurred in the fellowship of the church. The Corinthian church sent Paul a letter seeking clarification on certain issues that had become divisive. Paul's answers to this letter are prefaced with the phrase "Now concerning" beginning in 1 Corinthians 7:1. From this wealth of material, the Holy Spirit moved Paul to write a powerful letter of correction and instruction which will help us to answer some of our questions about spiritual gifts. Let's take a closer look at some of the distorted claims at Corinth.

We Are Spirituals

At the very core of the distorted view of spirituality in Corinth was the conviction on the part of some that they were "spiritual persons" in an elitist sense. "Spiritual persons" is my translation for a Greek word *pneumatikos* which is from the root word *pneuma* which means "spirit." This word occurs only twenty-four times in all the Pauline Epistles and fifteen of them are found in 1 Corinthians. For example, in 3:1 Paul stated that he could not refer to them as spiritual persons because they were bickering and fighting like children. It is obvious that they wanted to think they were spiritual, but their childish behavior said otherwise.

Paul began the discussion of spiritual gifts in 1 Corinthians 12 by answering a question from the Corinthians which must have implied that the spiritual gifts provided proof of their superior spirituality. "Doesn't the possession of spiritual gifts prove that we are spiritual persons?" After three chapters of corrective material Paul concluded the discussion with the warning: "If anyone thinks he is a prophet or spiritual, let him recognize that the things which I write to you are the Lord's commandment" (14:37). Certain showy spiritual gifts were at the very heart of the claim to be spiritual persons since they seemed to give verifiable proof of advanced spirituality.

It is unlikely that the spirituals were an organized group of persons in Corinth who opposed Paul's teaching. It doesn't even appear

that the persons involved had a clearly defined theological understanding of gifts. It seems more likely that their zeal for gifts came
from their fascination over the supernatural elements of Christian
conversion and a zest for religious ecstasy. They were like excited
children in a candy store.

In this letter Paul uses the word "zealous" (14:12) to describe the
youthful and often immature enthusiasm of this community. Their
misguided zeal led them to jealous bickering over religious leaders
(ch. 3). When we read 2 Corinthians, we notice that much of the
zealous boasting in leaders was related to their powerful gifts and
claimed visions. It is important to note that the Corinthians were
zealous for spiritual gifts (1 Cor. 12:31; 14:1, 12, 39). Paul could
say without reservation: "Since your are zealous of spiritual gifts
(14:12).

Paul was faced with a dilemma. He did not want to quench the
spiritual enthusiasm of these young believers, but he did want to correct it and redirect it toward more mature ends. My dad used to say
that as a pastor he wasn't sure whether it was easier to warm up a
spiritual corpse or cool down a zealot. Paul may have faced both
problems. While some were zealous for ecstatic religious experiences, the next powerful teacher, and their own rights; others had
responded with a calculated coolness to spiritual matters. We face
the same dilemma in the church today. Some folks flit from one
church to the next looking for the powerful preacher and most moving spiritual experience, while others don't want to talk about spiritual gifts for fear they might fall into the same pattern. Both are
errors which must be avoided.

Possession of certain dramatic gifts had given the spirituals a distorted image of themselves. They were, in their own opinion, spiritual giants. The word "to puff up" or "make arrogant" occurs only
seven times in the New Testament and six are found in 1 Corinthians.
The word "boast" is found fifty-three times in the New Testament,
and thirty-five of them are in this letter. Does that tell you anything
about the spirituals? They were puffed-up and they boasted because
of the gifts they possessed.

Thus although Paul did not face an organized group of opponents
in Corinth, he did face opposition. The spirituals, on the basis of
their gifts, had placed themselves and their leaders above Paul. In
their estimation he was lacking in wisdom and dramatic gifts. Paul
had to remind them that no matter how many teachers they might
have, he was still their father.

Did your parents ever leave you at home for a night or weekend when you were a teenager? They probably gave you a list of do's and don't's and then reminded you that they were trusting you to behave like a responsible and mature adult. Then they left! You were faced with the decision to live up to the expectations of your parents or to do your own thing. What would have happened if your parents had returned early? What would they have found? Would they have praised you for your behavior?

We face the same dilemma in the church today. Some folks flit from one church to the next looking for the powerful preacher and most moving spiritual experience, while others don't want to talk about spiritual gifts for fear they might fall into the same pattern. Both are errors which must be avoided.

Paul appealed to the Corinthians as a loving father (4:15) and issued a strong warning to those behaving disgracefully and arrogantly as if he were not returning to Corinth. The Corinthians had chosen to do their own thing rather than living up to the standards inherent in the gospel. Paul desired to come with a love and a gentle spirit, but feared that he might have to come as a disciplinarian. The Corinthians' disrespect for Paul's God-given leadership had led to a distorted view of themselves.

A Superstitious View of Grace

The spirituals had a crude and almost superstitious view of the spiritual life. In 10:3-4 Paul used the word "spiritual" three times when referring to the Israelites sojourn under Moses. The use of the word "baptized," the reference to the spiritual food and drink, and the ensuing discussion leads us to conclude that some in Corinth had a distorted view of baptism and the Lord's Supper, believing them to possess or impart some magical power. If you look at 1 Corinthians 1:10-17 you will notice that the issue of baptism was related to the divisions in Corinth. Apparently the Corinthians placed great significance on the person who had baptized them. Paul quickly reminds them that he had baptized very few of them so that no one could say they were baptized in his name.

In chapter 10 Paul compared their spiritual journey with that of the Israelites and reminded them that the Israelites were baptized into Moses. They had eaten spiritual food and had drunk spiritual drink, which was from the spiritual rock. Yet he concluded, because of their behavior, they were laid low in the wilderness. This example should serve as a stern warning against a spiritual arrogance based on baptism or participation in the Lord's table without a true life-changing experience with the Lord.

This magical view of the Lord's table had created critical problems in the community. It had led to the neglect of the true purpose and meaning of the love feast or fellowship meal which preceded the actual Lord's Supper. Thus, instead of creating fellowship and mutual concern, it had generated dissension. Some members came early and ate and drank their rich food without concern for poorer members of the fellowship who might go home hungry (11:17-34). Paul scolded them, telling them that when they gathered in this manner it was not to eat the Lord's Supper. A proper understanding of the Lord's table would lead to humility. It would cause them to discern the body of Christ incarnate in the fellowship of believers and, thus, seek to edify their fellow believer. It certainly would not produce arrogance and division.

This magical view of religion may at first seem foreign to us, but we must look at it more carefully for it still exists today. There are persons today who think that if they walk down the church aisle and are baptized that this act alone will put them right with God. This same superstitious attitude is detected when someone uses prayer or participation in the Lord's Supper or Mass as a religious talisman. Some individuals think wearing a cross or other religious jewelry offers some sort of divine protection. Still others think that an ecstatic religious experience assures them of greater spiritual position and authority. The belief that any religious activity, not accompanied by true repentance and conversion, can put a person in right standing with God demonstrates a magical view of the operation of grace. Any suggestion that some subjective religious or ecstatic experience, devoid of transformed behavior, makes one spiritually elite is religious superstition. These distorted views of grace are dangerous because they can inoculate us from true spirituality. A proper understanding of grace will cause us to seek God for God alone, not for any supposed favors or gifts that might be forthcoming.

We Have All Wisdom and Knowledge

Those who regarded themselves as spirituals claimed to possess special wisdom and knowledge. They believed that this wisdom gave them special insight into the mysteries of God's plan (2:6-9). Paul corrected the arrogant claim to a special wisdom by insisting that their wisdom was earthly wisdom and was foolishness before God (3:18-19). The most important corrective passage concerning wisdom is 2:6-16. Paul utilized the vocabulary of the spirituals to turn the table and demonstrate the content of true wisdom. True wisdom was not a private insight into the mysteries of God, but a clear understanding of the cross of Christ. The truly spiritual person would therefore recognize the things freely given by God (v. 12). This stress on recognizing God's gracious gifts is a primary corrective to the distorted view of the spirituals.

The spirituals apparently believed that Paul's teaching lacked deep spiritual insight, perhaps because he refused to base his teaching on visionary experiences. Paul, however, insisted that he shared spiritual things with spiritual men (v. 14). The corrective impact of this statement is obvious in 3:1 where Paul bluntly declared: "And I, brethren, could not speak to you as spiritual men, but as to men of flesh, as to babes in Christ."

Any preschool parent knows that three-year-old children go through the "why" stage. "Why is the sky blue?" is a question that can be answered many ways, but it would be foolish to launch a discussion with a three-year-old on how atmospheric conditions and the laws of science determine the sky's visual appearance. You do not want to discourage your child from asking questions, but giving him more than he can handle can be frustrating to both of you. It was not that Paul was unable to communicate true wisdom. The truth was the immaturity of the Corinthians had rendered them unable to comprehend the truly deep wisdom of the cross and the accompanying message of grace. A true understanding of the cross would eliminate all boasting. This, in turn, would stop the foolish strife created by their clamoring for one wise teacher after the other.

The spirituals believed that they possessed all knowledge and that this knowledge gave them special insight into the realities of Christian existence in the here and now. For example, on one occasion a claim to knowledge had been used to justify behavior which had created difficulties in the church concerning the eating of idol meat (see ch. 8). It is likely that Paul echoed the boast of the spirituals in verse 1; "We know that we all have knowledge." On the basis of this supposed knowledge, the spirituals had concluded that idols were nothing (v. 4), and thus decided that eating meat offered to idols was of no real consequence.

Paul countered by arguing that their knowledge was not as full as they thought. "If anyone supposes that he knows anything, he has not yet known as he ought to know" (v. 2). True knowledge, in contrast to their supposed knowledge, would have led to loving, edifying behavior toward the brethren. Their knowledge had resulted only in arrogance.

Once after a morning worship service a young stranger came up to me with a somewhat sheepish look. He said that he needed to talk with me right then. I stepped out of the flow of the traffic. He looked furtively over his shoulder like he was being followed and quietly informed me that he had a word for me from the Lord. He went on to explain that he enjoyed the service but that the Lord had instructed him to tell me that I should change the style of the worship service. I needed to allow for more freedom and spontaneous expression.

Any suggestion that some subjective religious or ecstatic experience, devoid of transformed behavior, makes one spiritually elite is religious superstition.

I asked him how often he had attended our church. He replied that this was his first visit. I told him that I found it somewhat surprising that the Lord would reveal such specialized knowledge to a complete stranger and fail to reveal it to me or any other responsible leader of the church. The difficulty with a mysterious word of knowledge or wisdom from the Lord is that it doesn't leave any room for discussion or contradiction.

I occasionally hear people complain when a pastor or television evangelist tells them that God has given him some particular vision that requires the entire church to respond. That leaves people in a quandary. They must accept this word and respond, or assume that the individual is mistaken or deceitful. In 2 Corinthians Paul finally conceded that he too had a visionary experience. Yet what he experienced in his vision was not communicable (12:1-4). Paul preferred to teach the intelligible and edifying message of the cross rather than impart some mystical message from the Lord. This distorted, mystical individualism is not the issue of spiritual gifts and has, in fact, caused many Christians to avoid the topic of gifts altogether.

We Already Reign

Some of the Corinthians were confused about issues related to the end of time. The word "spiritual" occurs four times in 1 Corinthians 15:44-46 in a manner which suggests that Paul had found it necessary to correct an *overrealized* eschatology. Don't quit on me! I know that's a new word for some of you. It means that some Corinthians believed that they already possessed all of the supernatural powers and blessings which heaven had to offer. To correct this false understanding Paul emphasized that the present body was "perishable," "sown in dishonor," "sown in weakness," "sown as a natural body." The spirituals, however, had no place for weakness or dishonor in this present existence.

The resurrection body, when it is given, will be "raised in glory," "raised in power," "raised a spiritual body." The spirituals were claiming that they already participated in the full glory and power of the Lord. Thus Paul conceded that there is "a spiritual body" (v. 44) but that is not first—it must follow the planting of the "natural" body (v. 46). Notice, too, that Paul concluded his discussion of the resurrection with a call to responsible Christian behavior in the present. "Therefore my beloved brethren, be steadfast, immovable, always abounding in the work of the Lord" (v. 58). To quote a popular little phrase: "The spirituals were so heavenly minded, they were no earthly good." Paul exhorted them to come back to earth and be steadfast in the work of the Lord.

Beware of the distorted view of spirituality which divorces itself from ethical behavior.

This mistaken understanding is actually reflected earlier in the letter where Paul summarized their belief about their own spiritual status: "You are already filled, you have already become rich, you have become kings without us" (4:8). Paul then contrasted their supposed present exalted status and greatness to the weakness and dishonor accorded the apostles. Lovingly he declared that he did not intend to shame them, but rather to admonish them as beloved children. Their arrogant assessment of themselves had actually caused them to neglect their God-given leaders such as Paul.

We find a similar distorted, overrealized eschatology today in a slightly more subtle form. One does not have to watch some of the televised worship services long to hear the preacher proclaim that the kingdom of God has already come in its full expression. He then assures the faithful that no Christian should be sick, suffer discouragement, or be poor. When such a condition does exist it must be the result of a lack of faith or understanding. Overrealized eschatology is at the heart of the health, wealth, and success gospel, and unfortunately it is often closely joined to a distorted view of gifts which are sought for their sign value and displayed arrogantly with little concern for the edification of the body. We too must heed the warning of Paul and see gifts in their proper context: in the body of Christ for the advancement of the gospel and the edification of believers.

We Don't Need Rules

Spiritual arrogance had caused the spirituals to have a warped understanding of freedom. They actually believed that their freedom had lifted them above normal rules of Christian morality, tradition, and sexual-role distinctions. Their slogan was quoted by Paul in 6:12 and 10:23: "All things are lawful." Their supposed exalted status had made irrelevant or even praiseworthy such bodily activities as sexual immorality.

Paul paid special attention to one flagrant case of immorality. One man was living with his stepmother in an incestuous relationship. Paul was horrified by the behavior. This affair was common knowledge in the Christian community. There had been no attempt to conceal it. On the contrary, some had boasted about it because it demonstrated how completely freed they were from the moral restrictions of conventional religious life (5:2-6). While at first we may be shocked to think that someone would boast concerning sexual sin, we still see people today who believe that their spirituality places them above reproof. Popular pastors and evangelists of differing denominations have been guilty of sexual sin. Some are truly repentant, but others seem to give the impression that such behavior does not truly affect them. Their superior gifts and advanced spirituality has placed them on another level than the average believer. Beware of the distorted view of spirituality which divorces itself from ethical behavior.

There are other curious problems that emerged from an arrogant insistence on freedom. The matter of eating meat idols offered to or attending a service at a pagan temple was, for some, an issue of freedom. They boasted that they had knowledge that the idol was nothing. Why shouldn't they eat the meat offered to the idol? So what if some of the weak believers were offended? That was their problem, and a sign of their weakness. The right of a woman to pray or prophesy in public had almost certainly become an issue of freedom for some of the spiritual women intent on making a public statement (ch. 11). Thus, they neglected the traditions of the church about proper decorum in the worship service. Paul corrected this distorted no-laws mentality with his insistence that the truly mature spiritual person would gladly surrender personal freedom for the sake of the gospel and the need of the brethren (ch. 9).

Contemporary Images

It would be easy to leave the discussion of distorted images in the past, but we would gain little from our study if we did. Where do we confront distorted images which can hamper us in discovering our God-given uniqueness?

Some of the distorted images that hinder our development come from early childhood experiences. Children who have been verbally or physically abused often blame themselves rather than the bigger person who was the actual cause of the abuse. The abuse may have been a simple but stinging "one-liner" intended to make us toe the line. Even now as an adult all our accomplishments can't seem to erase the one-liner from our childhood that keeps repeating like a broken record.

On other occasions we may have a distorted image caused by unreal expectations. We may have created these expectations for ourselves, or they may have come from a parent or teacher. Perhaps we could never make the kind of grades that an older sibling made or excel in sports like another family member. We may have grown up surrounded by an array of trophies but not one of them had our name on it. We childishly and inappropriately concluded that we were no good. These distorted images can continue to cause us to view ourselves from a negative perspective.

Other distorted images may come from false ideas about success or greatness. Many of the "image enhancement programs" available today are based on an inadequate foundation. Following popular philosophy, some persons believe that financial success, physical prowess or beauty, a powerful position, or the right friends guarantee a healthy self-image. Health spas are sprouting like mushrooms; visible images of success are eagerly sought and purchased; the market place has become a cut-throat arena for the upwardly mobile; and yet people are still recoiling under the heavy weight of self-doubt and inferiority. In spite of all the trappings of success and multitude of positive image seminars, people feel empty inside. Distorted images must be honestly confronted and rejected in the context of redemptive community.

Once Jesus compared the Pharisees to white-washed sepulchers. They were painted up on the outside, but empty on the inside. Do you ever feel that way? A permanent change of our self-image requires that we change from within. That begins when we accept Christ and have our inner person changed. That's what the new birth is all about. Paul wrote that the person in Christ "is a new creature; the old things passed away; behold, new things have come" (2 Cor. 5:17). Once the inner transformation has occurred we have the real foundation for building a strong new self-image. (See appendix A.) Yet we must volitionally and daily refuse to listen to that old distorted view and accept the affirmation of our heavenly Father that we are His unique creation. This book is intended to help you to do just that.

God made you and then He paid the price to allow you to become His child. That makes me realize what incredible worth I have. God Himself paid the price to enable me to be a child of God. As such, I am a special creation. No one is quite like me. Praise God!

Reflections in the Mirror

1. The difficulties Paul encountered in Corinth can be traced to a spiritual enthusiasm which did not have any developed theological system or any real unity. It was an immature reaction to spiritual matters which had, no doubt, been fed by various wise teachers. The one undergirding theological foundation was the mistaken idea that the full expression of the kingdom had already been made available

to the believer. Do you think that you've arrived spiritually, or are you anxious to discover what God can do with your life?

2. Spiritual gifts were central to this immature spirituality because they offered verifiable proof of one's advanced spiritual maturity. Paul wrote to correct a distorted view of spiritual maturity based on the possession of certain spectacular gifts, while, at the same time, he offered a more balanced and biblical view. Gifts are the manifestation of grace and provide no basis for spiritual arrogance. This being the case, the more edifying gifts, not the spectacular ones, should be eagerly sought. Are you willing to develop any gift God has given you regardless of how "spiritual" it may seem?

3. Paul's primary correctives are grace and love. The truly spiritual person will recognize that all is of grace and therefore will find no grounds for boasting in any gift. Second, the spiritual person will determine his/her behavior by love, which leads to actions which edify the members of the body. What actions and attitudes do you manifest that are destructive to your church fellowship? Are you willing to leave those behind and seek to edify the body?

4. We too must avoid distorted images of spiritual gifts if we are to discover our God-given selves in a way that will develop a healthy biblical self-image and enable us to edify the body. We must lay aside the mistaken notions that:

   a) Spiritual gifts are proof that one is more spiritually mature than another believer.
   b) Religious activities have a magical power which makes us immune to the power of sin.
   c) We have all wisdom and knowledge and that such knowledge places us above others, making us spiritually arrogant.
   d) We have already arrived spiritually and that we have escaped the bounds of earthly constraints.
   e) We don't have to obey the rules that govern community relationships.

5. Are you carrying any distorted views from childhood or your own spiritual training that could inhibit your ability to discover and use your spiritual gift?

   a) Acknowledge the distorted and debilitating images from your past. List them on a separate piece of paper.
   b) Agree with God that they are distorted views and do not come from your Father. Tear the list up.

c) Ask the Father to remove these distorted images and allow you to see yourself as He sees you.

d) Start by memorizing these affirming verses:

- Genesis 1:27—"And God created [insert your name] in His own image"
- Proverbs 3:26—"For the Lord will be your confidence"
- John 14:12—"Truly, truly, I say to you, he who believes in Me, the works that I do shall he do also; and greater works than these shall he do; because I go to the Father."
- Romans 8:32—"He who did not spare His own Son, but delivered Him up for us all, how will He not also with Him freely give us all things?"
- 1 Corinthians 12:7—"But to each one [insert your name in place of "each one"] is given the manifestation of the Spirit for the common good"
- 1 Corinthians 12:18—"But now God has placed the members, each one of them [insert your name "for each one of them"], in the body, just as He desired."

A More Accurate Reflection: Redefining Spiritual Gifts

It's time to escape the house of mirrors and wipe off any fog that might distort the image in the mirror before us. Just what does the Bible teach about spiritual gifts and how can I discover mine? The questions are certainly in the right order. We must first have a clear biblical understanding of spiritual gifts before we are prepared to begin the discovery process.

- What gifts are available?
- What is their value?
- Do I seek them or do they just appear?
- Can they be developed?
- Can they be controlled?

These are all questions that can and should be answered before we begin the discovery process. We will find the majority of our answers in 1 Corinthians 12—14.

Much is at stake in the discovery of our true giftedness. I've already suggested that our personal understanding will be greatly enhanced as we discover our unique giftedness. Our gifts determine, to a great extent, where we will find purpose and make a meaningful contribution in life. If we are working in our area of giftedness, we're going to feel fulfilled and satisfied. This creates a healthy self-image. Our gifts also will tell us where we can make the greatest contribution through the church for the cause of Christ. And since our work through the body of Christ, His church, will impact eternity itself, this is the most critical work we can do. Review the seven building blocks to a positive self-image (p. 12) and you will note that we are certainly moving in the right direction in our pilgrimage to discover our gifts.

The Common Work of the Spirit

The little phrase, "Now concerning" in 1 Corinthians 12:1 alerts us to the fact that Paul was responding to an inquiry from the Corinthian community. It seems that the various teachers who had visited Corinth since Paul's departure had created confusion about gifts. It would be helpful and fascinating to have a copy of the letter the Corinthians wrote, wouldn't it? We would like to know the actual questions and how they were worded. We can get some idea about the question based on the answer which follows.

The word translated "spiritual gifts" (v. 1) in the *New American Standard Version* could also be rendered "spiritual persons." I think that "spiritual persons" and "spiritual gifts" were so closely connected in the Corinthians' minds that Paul used the word in such a way as to imply both. Perhaps the question could be restated as follows: "Don't the spiritual gifts prove that we are spiritual persons?"

First Corinthians 12—14 answers this simple question. Paul first redefined and broadened the understanding of the work of the Spirit and spiritual gifts (ch. 12). Second, he provided a positive new definition of what it truly meant to be a spiritual person (ch. 13). We could say that he gave a different answer to the question; "What proves that I possess the Spirit?" Finally he supplied clear guidelines for seeking and using spiritual gifts for the good of the community (ch. 14).

We can relate to the implications of the Corinthian question. Because of the resurgence and popularity of the charismatic movement, many of us have encountered well-meaning folk who have had what they consider to be a profound religious experience which involved spiritual gifts. They often testify to this experience by pointing to an objective sign, frequently the gift of tongues, to prove that they have had a valid experience. Some are zealous for us to share in this experience. These evangelists for spiritual things can leave us with the impression that we're really missing out if we turn our back on their offer. Worse yet, they may suggest that we do not have or are not baptized in the Spirit unless we speak in tongues. Some believers come away from these encounters feeling like second-class Christians, another blow to their already pummeled self-esteem.

You begin to think; *Could they be right? They do seem to be more on fire than I am. Must I speak in tongues to discover the fullness of the Spirit and uncover my true giftedness?* The answer is no! Tongues are not required for gift discovery as Paul made abundantly clear in

12:30. Relax and keep reading. Allow the Holy Spirit to guide you in your discovery of your gifted self. Our Father knows how to give good gifts.

Our gifts determine where we will find purpose and make a meaningful contribution in life.

I am appreciative of the charismatic movement because it has helped us to look again at the ministry of the Holy Spirit and at the spiritual gifts. It has caused us to reevaluate our spiritual walk and to seek a deeper experience with the Lord. I honestly do not remember a great deal of teaching on the work of the Holy Spirit while I was growing up in my Baptist tradition. We must understand the ministry of the Spirit and walk daily in His empowering. The Holy Spirit is the source of spiritual life and provides the empowering for ministry. The impotence of the average Christian and the average church is directly related to the failure to appropriate the empowering of the Spirit of God. We can heartily agree with our charismatic friends on these matters. This does not mean that we should accept uncritically everything the charismatic community teaches. If they repeat theological errors corrected by Paul in 1 Corinthians, we must accept Paul's inspired teaching.

We're hardly prepared for Paul's first words in response to their question about spiritual gifts/persons. Why did Paul remind them of their idolatrous past and then introduce the shocking phrase "Jesus is accursed"? (12:3) As you read this letter don't forget the historical situation or the present context. Since the possession of the Spirit and the resulting spiritual gifts was at the heart of the Corinthian difficulties, Paul focused first on the *common* work of the Spirit. By *common,* I mean the ministry of the Spirit which all believers share equally.

In the first thirteen verses of chapter 12 there are twelve references to the Spirit. This discovery is even more impressive when you notice that the Spirit is not mentioned in Romans 12 or Ephesians 4, the two other primary passages about spiritual gifts. The Corinthians were obsessed with proving their spirituality and, therefore, Paul first had to correct their aberrant view of the Spirit's work by underlining the work of the Spirit in all Christians.

Why did Paul use the blunt and unexpected "Jesus is accursed"? You might be thinking it is incomprehensible that a Christian could say "Jesus is accursed" when speaking under the inspiration of the Spirit. You are absolutely correct, for the ministry of the Spirit is to witness to Christ, not to curse Him. Then why mention a truth so obvious it need not be stated? Because it is equally impossible for the Christian to say "Jesus is Lord" except by the Holy Spirit. We might then loosely paraphrase this verse: "It is *obvious* to you that no one could curse Jesus when speaking in the Spirit; in the same manner, it should be equally *obvious* that every person who truly confesses that Jesus is Lord is a spiritual person!" The confession "Jesus is Lord" was the earliest Christian confession. It was repeated at baptism as a verbal confession of salvation. Thus these words would have been etched in the memory of all the believers in Corinth.

We have the popular equivalent to this kind of argumentation today. Someone standing in the rain declares, "It's raining!" That observation is usually followed by a friendly barb like: "Really, Sherlock?" We mean that the evidence of the rain is so obvious to everyone it need not be mentioned. In the same manner Paul used the obvious—no one could curse Jesus speaking by the Spirit of God—to dramatize an equally obvious truth—no one can say Jesus is Lord except by the Spirit. Thus Paul's first corrective was to refute the exclusivistic claim by the spirituals that they alone possessed the Spirit. Paul appealed to the most fundamental truth of the Christian experience—salvation through the work of the Spirit—to prove his point.

The Holy Spirit is the source of spiritual life and provides the empowering for ministry.

This introductory corrective ought to serve as a comfort to those who have been told that they do not have the Spirit unless they speak in tongues. You cannot be saved without the work of the Spirit. It should also serve as a warning to those who have become spiritually arrogant because they have been taught that their possession of a certain gift makes them more spiritual than those without the gift. This teaching leads to unhealthy conclusions on the part of both parties and destroys the fellowship of the church. This danger existed in Corinth and it still rears its divisive head today.

Paul's singular purpose in these first three verses was to clearly establish the fact that every believer is a spiritual person since the basic confession "Jesus is Lord" cannot be uttered except by the work of the Holy Spirit. The reference to the confession "Jesus is Lord" brings the discussion of gifts within the perspective of the Lordship of Christ. In is only in the context of personal relationship with Christ and thus the common possession of the Spirit that Paul could put forward his corrective teaching on spiritual gifts.

The common work of the Spirit is further emphasized by the repetition of phrases such as "same Spirit," "the one Spirit," and "one and the same Spirit" in verses 4, 9, and 11. Verses 7 and 11 frame the first gift list and demonstrate the central purpose of the discussion. "But to each one is given the manifestation of the Spirit for the common good. But *one and the same* Spirit works all these things, distributing to *each one* individually just as He wills" (emphasis added). The emphasis on the common work of the Spirit is made more explicitly when Paul repeats *Spirit* four times in the gift list (vv. 8-10) in phrases such as "according to the same Spirit" and "by the one Spirit." This section of chapter 12 is linked to the body imagery in verses 14–24 by the important reminder: "For by *one Spirit we all* were baptized into one body, ... and *we all* were made to drink of *one Spirit*" (v. 13, emphasis added). In case there was any doubt Paul assured them that every Christian in the Corinthian community was baptized into one body by the one Spirit. This baptism of the Spirit is the incorporation of the believer into the body of Christ which occurs at the moment of conversion, when one confesses "Jesus is Lord."

The Umbrella of Grace

Now that Paul had clearly established that the Spirit works in all persons in their conversion, he moved a step further to assure the Corinthians that *all believers* possessed gifts for ministry. Verse 7 could hardly be more pointed: "But to each one is given the manifestation of the Spirit for the common good." The possession of gifts for ministry did not prove that a person was spiritual in a boastful sense. On the contrary, it demonstrated that all believers alike had received grace. Accordingly, Paul introduced a new word to describe the spiritual gifts. The spirituals had preferred the word *pneumatikon* (v. 1) which comes from the Greek word for *spirit*. This word can be translated "manifestation of the Spirit." In verse 4 Paul answered their question about spiritual gifts, but he substituted the word *charismata*. This word comes from the Greek root word for *grace*. This term should be translated "manifestation of grace."

The substitution of terms is an important change for it brings the discussion of gifts under the corrective umbrella of grace, a prominent theme of this letter. Paul was making clear that the "gifts for ministry" are the result of God's grace in the life of every believer, and therefore they offer no grounds for spiritual pride.

The baptism of the Spirit is the incorporation of the believer
into the body of Christ which occurs
at the moment of conversion.

Think of it this way. Your daughter is turning six years old. You've planned a big party, made a cake, and invited family and friends to celebrate this occasion. That child has every right in the world to be proud of the fact that she is now six, big enough to start school and enter a new phase of her life. However, she herself had nothing to do with the fact that she is six! As we discover our spiritual gifts, we can be proud of how God lets us use and develop those gifts, but we must realize we have nothing to do with actually having them and they are not a result of a level of spirituality.

If the possession of gifts proves anything, it proves that God is gracious. Gifts are by their very nature "gifts of grace" and therefore they prove nothing about the possessor but everything about the giver. God is gracious to gift His church to accomplish every task to which He calls it.

This Greek term *charismata* is the word from which we get the English word *charismatic*. Often when I hear the word *charismatic* used today, it is used somewhat like the spirituals at Corinth used *pneumatika*. It is sometimes used to refer to persons who claim to manifest certain gifts which prove their status as spiritual persons. This word has become divisive in our day, when, in fact, it was used by Paul in a corrective manner to stop all spiritual boasting and to heal the divisions in the Corinthian community.

Paul began this letter with the corrective of grace. In his prayer of thanksgiving in 1:4-9, he thanked God "for the grace of God which was given you in Christ Jesus" (v. 1). He then proceeded to talk about the abundance of their gifts. The corrective of "grace" is found in verses 27-31 where Paul insisted that human boasting was excluded before God because He was the very source of life. Thus if we want to boast we should boast in the Lord. In chapter 2 Paul contrasted the "wisdom" of the spirituals with the true wisdom of God. Paul concluded that genuine spiritual persons are those who have received the Spirit who is from God: "That we might know the things freely given to us by God" (v. 12). Notice that true spirituality makes us aware of the graciousness of all of life.

Gifts are by their very nature "gifts of grace" and therefore they prove nothing about the possessor but everything about the giver.

The grace corrective is central to Paul's teaching in chapter 3. Paul could not refer to them as spiritual persons but as babes because of their strife and arrogant exalting of one leader over another. The root cause of their strife was their lack of *true* spiritual wisdom. Otherwise they would have understood that Paul and Apollos were just men, servants through whom God worked. Paul and Apollos had different ministries, but God caused the growth (v. 6). Paul laid the foundation but that in itself was "According to the grace of God which was given to me" (v. 10). The corrective of 4:7 is even more pointed: "For who regards you as superior? And what do you have that you did not receive? But if you did receive it, why do you boast as if you had not received it?"

Before we go further in our search to discover our gifted image in Christ, let's make sure that we understand the significance of the grace corrective. Whatever gift or gifts we possess, they do not provide a grounds for boasting. They offer no proof of our spiritual greatness, but they do offer abundant proof that our God has graciously gifted us to accomplish the purpose for which He created us. You can be assured that as a believer you have been graced by God. You are uniquely gifted for creative ministry to which He has called you. You have inherent worth at the hands of your Creator.

The Variety of Gifts

Even the casual reader of 1 Corinthians 12 will notice the emphasis on variety. "There are varieties of gifts" (v. 4), "varieties of ministries" (v. 5), "varieties of effects" (v. 6). These three words view the gifts for ministry from different perspectives. "Gifts" emphasizes the graciousness of the Spirit in the giving and thus excludes boasting. "Ministries" indicates that the gifts cannot be regarded as spiritual privileges, but are to be viewed as God-given means for service and thus must be surrendered to His lordship. Jesus' emphasis on service must have had a profound impact on the early disciples. Finally, "effects" exalts God as the source and energizer of all activities of service accomplished within the Christian community. These three words provide a crescendo which draws attention to God as the ultimate source of all gifts.

True spirituality makes us aware of the graciousness
of all of life.

The repetition of "varieties" contrasted with the repetition of "same" ("same Spirit, . . . same Lord, . . . same God") impressively lays the foundation for Paul's insistence that variety and unity are not mutually exclusive. They are both divinely given. The spirituals, by placing a premium on a few miraculous "sign" gifts, had actually caused a neglect of the diversity of gifts available to the Christian community. This same thing happens today when we allow folk who have become overzealous over a few gifts to keep us from truly seeking to discover and use our own spiritual gifts.

Verse 7 serves as a bridge between the emphasis on variety and the first list of gifts. "But to each one is given the manifestation of the Spirit for the common good." Two points are made, with the emphasis on the second. First, Paul emphatically declared that *each* Christian was given a manifestation of the Spirit. Second, no one was given a manifestation of the Spirit for personal gratification but only "for the common good." This was suggested by the use of "ministries" in verse 5, but is stated here in unequivocal terms. Gifts are not given to a few spiritually elite for self-glorification but to each believer for the good of the body. Both of these points will be illustrated through the use of the imagery of the body.

Now we come to the first listing of gifts. Since there are several different gift lists in Paul's letters, we know that this list was not intended to be comprehensive. Yet it does not seem likely that the gifts listed here were chosen haphazardly. When we look at the list as a whole several characteristics emerge.

1. These gifts would have been prominent in the worship service.

2. They are the gifts most frequently referred to by people today as "miraculous."

3. Many of the gifts are directly related to speech and revelation.

4. It follows that we would find little continuity between these gifts and any abilities possessed before one becomes a Christian.

It may seem curious that Paul included such a "miraculous" list at the point. As we have already seen, a part of the Corinthian dilemma was that not all the believers in Corinth possessed such miraculous expressions of the Spirit as we find listed here. It may seem at first that Paul has virtually retreated from his position that all are gifted and has agreed with their emphasis on a few miraculous gifts.

Whatever gift or gifts we possess, they do not provide a grounds for boasting. They offer no proof of our spiritual greatness, but they do offer abundant proof that our God has graciously gifted us to accomplish the purpose for which He created us.

I do think it is a safe assumption that this list clearly reflects the gifts most eagerly desired by the spirituals in Corinth. A glance at 1:5-7 and 13:1-3 will further illustrate the exaggerated interest in a few sign gifts. These gifts were audible and dramatic, easy to display in the worship service, and thus provided ready proof of one's spirituality.

While it may appear that this list is a concession to the spirituals, it is in fact an important plank in Paul's corrective. Paul wanted to demonstrate one truth ignored by the spirituals—a variety of gifts were already present in Corinth. The spirituals had not been interested in the variety of gifts already present because they were uninterested in service. They had viewed their spiritual manifestations as miraculous signs of spirituality. They hadn't really noticed that by the use of tongues, prophecy, and other gifts they were already exercising a variety of gifts. Having now established the principle of variety by listing their chosen gifts, Paul was prepared to expand the scope of gifted ministry by including functions not previously considered by the spirituals. This he will do in the second listing of gifts found in verses 28-30 of chapter 12.

Gifts are not given to a few spiritually elite for self-glorification but to each believer for the good of the body.

The Picture of the Human Body

The human body is a miraculous instrument, particularly when all parts work in synch. Yet when one part fails to perform for any reason, the whole body is affected. As a child, I seemed to have a knack for stumping my big toe. I can still remember the pain that shot through my body when I drove my toe into the raised section of the sidewalk. Yet I pretended to be a macho kid and would choke back the tears and continue on my way thinking, *It's only one toe.* After limping down the street for awhile, I would begin to notice that my thigh and hip had started to throb with pain because of my awkward gait. The pain then began to crawl up my spine, and I began to hurt all over. All because of one big toe!

Paul drew attention to the human body to illustrate both the need for variety and mutual care. For churches to work properly and minister effectively, all the body parts must work in harmony and demonstrate care for one another. The picture of the body will not only help us to understand the correctives needed in Corinth, but also those needed in our churches today.

In this section Paul moved his argument for an expanded definition of gifts a step further. Paul wanted to establish five distinctive points through the extended metaphor of the body. 1) There is one body, 2) with diversely functioning members, 3) sovereignly designed, 4) with no useless appendages to, 5) provide mutual care to all the members of the body.

All Members Belong to the One Body

Paul first called attention to the makeup of the physical body. All the members of the human body, whatever their differences in function, belong to the one body. The conclusion to verse 12 is abrupt: "so also is Christ." It was intended to direct the reader's attention from the human illustration to the spiritual truth concerning the Christian community. He could have said, "So also is the church," but he more pointedly concluded, "So also is Christ," because the church is more than the mere assemblage of members, it is the body of Christ.

When you were saved you were immediately included in the body of Christ. You may not feel like you belong anywhere. Perhaps you don't belong to any club, fraternal group, or organization. You do, however, belong to the body of Christ. No other single organization on earth is as significant as the community of faith. You don't have to feel left out any longer.

There is one body, with diversely functioning members, sovereignly designed, with no useless appendages, to provide mutual care to all the members of the body.

The variety of members are molded into one body by the action of the Spirit: "For by one Spirit we were all baptized into one body" (v. 13). This is the final reference to the Spirit in this chapter, and it is the pivotal point which enabled Paul to move his teaching on gifts beyond the limited understanding of the spirituals. Remember, that throughout this first section Paul has focused on the work of the Spirit which all believers share in common. The Spirit enabled *every* believer to confess "Jesus is Lord," and He dispensed gifts to each as He willed. In this verse Paul took the next logical step by emphasizing that the *one Spirit* had brought *all believers* into a single body. The emphasis changes from the individual work of the Spirit to His corporate work of making one body from the diverse members. This is wholly consistent with Paul's insistence that the manifestations of the Spirit were given to *each believer* for the good of the *whole body*. Paul first affirmed the individual's participation in the Spirit (echoing the emphasis of the spirituals) in order to share a more mature understanding of the Spirit's work. The *one Spirit* incorporates *all* true believers into *one body*. The spirituals had clamored for the gifts in an immature individualistic fashion as a sign of spiritual achievement and had totally neglected their true purpose.

The church is more than the mere assemblage of members, it is the body of Christ.

This same error is repeated today anytime an individual's purpose in seeking spiritual gifts is not related to the good of the whole. When people come to me wanting help in discovering their gifts, I usually inquire concerning their motives. Is this a spiritual badge you need? Are you looking for prestige or power over others? Are you seeking gifts because you've been intimidated by a well-meaning friend who has suggested you may be lacking in spirituality? Or do you want to find your place of service in the body of Christ? If your motive is other than service oriented, if your focus is other than the good of the body, then gifts will provide for you only a distorted image of spirituality. If, however, your motives are pure, the discovery and employment of your gifts will provide a true biblical image of your self-worth. They will enable you to discover your God-given purpose.

An interesting use of mirrors is the rearview mirror in your car. If you have ever gotten something in your eye while driving, or if you are one of those females who puts on makeup at stoplights or a male who shaves on the way to work, you know that you have to physically adjust your mirror to see yourself. If the rearview mirror is facing you, it forfeits its intended purpose. It can only fulfill its primary function if it is focused away from the user! If you desire or use gifts to focus on yourself, they are not fulfilling their purpose. God gives the gifts to glorify Himself and edify the body of Christ. You can only use them to their fullest potential if they are focused away from you and focused on God's purpose through His church.

When you were saved you were immediately included in the body of Christ. No other organization on earth is as significant. You don't have to feel left out any longer.

The One Body Is Made up of Diverse Members

The uniqueness of Christian unity is that it still preserves individuality. Paul's reference to various national and social groups represented in the Christian community clearly illustrated diversity. "Jews or Greeks, . . . slaves or free" (v. 13), were all baptized into one body and made to drink of one Spirit. The reference to the common experience of water baptism was not simply a nostalgic reminder of a past event, but was intended to impress upon the Corinthians the ability of the Spirit to bring unity in diversity. Ironically, by the zeal to possess only the more miraculous gifts, the spirituals had ignored the God-given variety necessary for unity.

To establish this point Paul turned to an extended illustration based on the working of the human body. Paul's use of this familiar image was striking because the examples often verged on the ridiculous. "For the body is not one member, but many" (v. 14) sets the tone of the passage and shows that Paul was concerned about the individualistic view of the spirituals. The zeal of the spirituals to be alike in possessing the miraculous gifts had resulted in the failure to appreciate the diversity of the body and in turn had led to rampant individualism. This caused them to act or speak without considering the impact of their actions on other body members.

The foot and the ear are first pictured as arguing that they are not a part of the body because they are not the hand or the eye. We may consider our foot to be less glamorous than our hand or our ear to be less vital than our eye, but, in truth, all parts are equally vital. The parts differ because the body demands diversity in function for unity in action.

This argument reminds us of the childhood squabbles that occurred when we were going out for recess at school. "If I can't pitch, I'm not going to play." "That's not fair; she always plays the center position." Sounds similar to our church games doesn't it? "If I can't teach, I'll leave the church!" "She always gets the lead solo in the cantata! She has only been a member for a short time; she doesn't deserve such an important part." Statements like these demonstrate a failure to understand the purpose and function of the gifts. Ministry opportunities are not awards for longevity or faithful attendance. Because you can't sing or teach doesn't mean that you are less important to the function of the body. We're not in competition with one another in the body of Christ. We are members of the same body, and we are called to serve according to our gifts for the good of the whole. As the ear is no less a part of our human body than the eye, so the secretary is no less a part of the church body than the soloist.

If your motive is other than service oriented, then gifts will provide for you only a distorted image of spirituality.

If you are seeking an impressive gift to prove to yourself your spiritual worth, you're still visiting the house of mirrors hoping that the exaggerated image in the mirror will remain when you walk away. Your importance is not determined by the visibility or the spectacular impact of your gift. It is determined by the very fact that you have been uniquely gifted for service to the body by God Himself. You don't have to be a star soloist or skillful teacher to be important to the life of the body. The focus of the spiritual gifts is on *function* and not *status*.

The Body Is Sovereignly Designed

In verses 17-19 Paul asked three questions which frame the central idea that God has sovereignly designed the body. When we link the questions together, it sounds like this: "If all the body were an eye. If all the body were an ear. If they were all one part?" When I read these verses as a child, I could picture this huge eyeball rolling down the road. Impressive but ludicrous picture! A huge eye would be of no value without connection to the body. The central verse in this passage is verse 18, a verse which should be underlined in your Bible and your heart. "But now God has placed the members, each one of them, in the body, just as He desired." In case you think that this verse still applies to everyone but you, notice that the emphatic "each one of them" actually interrupts the flow of the sentence.

Your importance is not determined by the visibility or the spectacular impact of your gift. It is determined by the very fact that you have been uniquely gifted for service to the body by God Himself.

There Are No Useless Parts in God's Design

The body imagery is pressed even further with the Corinthian situation clearly in mind. The spirituals were saying, either verbally or by their actions, that they had no need for other Christians, particularly those who were weaker or without honor. The arrogant spirituals believed they were especially honored by God and that the inferior members were of little use; in fact they might be deemed a hindrance.

Let this idea sink in! *You* have been placed in the body of Christ by design. *You* are exactly who God designed you to be. Your function is vital to the body because God made you just as He desired. Without you the body would be lacking. You are the created and God is the Creator. Our primary point of reference should then be that we are pleasing to our Creator. When you complete a project, the essential question is whether the created object pleases you and serves your purpose. Thus, with us, the primary question concerning our giftedness and service is not worth in the world's eyes, but worth in God's eyes. God's Word says that He placed each one of us in the body as He desired. If you are serving where He placed you, then you are pleasing to your Creator. You don't have to sing the solo or be a deacon to be valuable to your church and your Creator; you need only serve in the area of your giftedness. God's mirror reflects true value.

Several years ago Greg Louganis was at the pinnacle of his athletic prowess and at the top of the diving world. He was the best there was. Nonetheless, at times he did not perform well. At one point in his career he went through a serious slump. He even had a dangerous accident when his head hit the high platform while performing a dive. The reporters speculated about his ability to come back and perform well. One reporter asked Greg what was his last thought as he stood motionless on that high diving platform. I'll never forget his simple but profound response. He said, "My last thought is that whether I hit the dive correctly or not, my mom will still love me." Great perspective! The judges might mark him down, but his relationship with his mom would still be solidly in place. Your gifts are grace expressions from the Father, and you're not being graded on performance but empowered for faithful service, and no matter how you hit the dive, He'll still love you.

You *are exactly who God designed you to be. Your function is vital to the body because God made you just as He desired.*

When I was a young child, my dad took me to most of the local high school football games. He used these Friday night outings not only to teach me about football, a passion of his, but also about life. I can still vividly remember one year that the team had a particularly skilled quarterback. The only problem was that he knew he was gifted and constantly reminded others of that fact. He was cocky! You could see it in his disregard for other team members. You could detect it when he was interviewed after the game and clearly implied that if other team members would play up to his standards the team would win more games. It was apparent that he viewed the linemen as unskilled hulks who did little more than provide a stage for the display of his spectacular gifts.

What happened during that season was not commendable on anyone's part, but perhaps it taught the quarterback a lesson. My dad noticed and pointed out to me that the linemen often stood huddled on the sidelines conversing while the quarterback walked proudly back and forth in view of the crowd. Apparently these meetings were used to devise their strategy. If this quarterback could do it all, if they were mere useless appendages, they would let him have his desire. Every once in awhile, by prearranged agreement, they would all miss their blocking assignment. This always seemed to happen when the quarterback called a play designed to showcase his own talents.

Needless to say the quarterback spent considerable time observing the stars from flat of his back. Perhaps he learned the hard way that there are no useless appendages.

In order to appreciate what Paul meant, we must understand that "weaker," "unseemly," and "less honorable" (vv. 22-23) do not refer to actual body appendages such as feet or internal organs, but they refer to other members of the community as viewed by the spirituals. Several passages in 1 Corinthians use similar terms. In 1:26-28 Paul reminded the Corinthians that when they came to Christ not many of them were "wise," "mighty," or "noble." Clearly some Corinthians now believed that they were all these things. Paul concluded that God had chosen the weak to shame the strong. If they were anything, it was only because of the work of grace in redemption and thus "Let him who boasts, boast in the Lord" (v. 31).

A more pointed passage is 4:8-13. The possessions of the miraculous gifts had made the spirituals feel superior to their fellow believers and even to the apostles. The spirituals, in their own distorted view, were "already filled," they were "rich," and reigned like "kings." In contrast, the apostles were last of all, like men condemned to death. "We are fools for Christ's sake, but ye are wise in Christ; we are weak, but ye are strong; ye are honorable, but we are despised" (v. 10, KJV). One doesn't have to read too closely to hear the ironic edge to that verse.

The same type of irony is present in 12:21-26. Although the spirituals judged themselves to be most valuable and important, the opposite was true. Those members they considered to be weaker are necessary and honored. Those parts of the body which we think to be less honorable by human standards are invested with greater honor and treated with greater modesty. Nearly everyone has some body part which they think to be their least attractive feature. You may think your nose too long, your hips too large, or your eyes too dull. When you put on your clothes, comb your hair, or put on makeup, you actually pay the greater attention to your least flattering body member. In your attempt to hide or decorate this unseemly member, you give it more abundant honor.

Paul rejected the spirituals' criteria for evaluating which gifts were most honorable. They had chosen the most visible or audible gifts for selfish reasons. Since the sole purpose of the gifts was to build up the body of Christ, the true criterion for the greatness of any gift would be its usefulness to the body of Christ. Paul clearly expressed this in verse 25: "That there should be no division in the body, but that the members should have the same care for one another." Thus their distorted concept of spirituality and gifts had led them to childishly seek the showier gifts without due concern for their given purpose. This, in turn, had led only to division in the body.

I wonder if Paul had in mind the teaching of Jesus in which the order of popular evaluation was radically reversed. Jesus taught that the servant, the one deemed to be the lowest, was, in fact, the highest in the kingdom. Those who desire true spiritual greatness must choose to become servants. Paul verified this reversal of values by stating that God Himself has "composed" (v. 24) or "blended together" the body so as to give more abundant honor to that member which lacked.

The true criterion for the greatness of any gift is its usefulness to the body of Christ.

Ask yourself:

- Do you desire to discover your gifts so that you can find your proper place of service?
- Do you truly believe that servanthood is the highest form of service?
- Does your church have people lined up for those unheralded areas of service?
- Would you be disappointed if you were to discover that you were gifted to be a helper and not a leader?
- Could it be that we have all been slightly infected with the disease of the spirituals in our preference for the more visible and honorable areas of ministry?

Slam dunking over Michael Jordan is a much more appealing image than wrapping Michael's ankles.

Paul did not desire to discredit the spirituals; he only wanted to redirect their zeal for spiritual gifts away from ego gratification and towards a more productive end. Gifts for them were signs of their heavenly status, not gifts of grace enabling them to care for the body.

The Design of the Body Requires Mutual Care

The picture of the human body reminds us that all the members of the one body are interdependent. Because the proper working of the body demands unity, there must be no discord. Division in the church is not simply wrong, it is disastrous because it inhibits the proper working of the body. Could you imagine the embarrassing results if your brain thought one thing and your mouth said another? What if one foot decided to go left while the other went right? Like the awkward gait of the little boy with a stumped toe, the church with discord limps ineffectively from one task to the next. The mission of the church is too important for us to allow discord to creep in and siphon away our power.

When the body functions properly, with all gifted members in harmonious relationship, there will be mutual "care" (v. 25) and total empathy (v. 26). We have already noted several occasions where mutual care was conspicuously lacking in Corinth. Some had, through their gift of knowledge, determined that meat offered to idols was acceptable. They had not, however, considered the effect their eating might have on a weaker brother. The celebration of the Lord's Supper was another prime example where mutual care was lacking.

Paul took the theme of mutual care one step further. As members of the same body, we are so closely bound together that we actually share the same feelings. What causes joy for one member delights the whole body. When one member suffers, the entire body hurts. Most of us do a better job empathizing with those who suffer than we do rejoicing with those who are honored. How do you react when someone else gets the part in the Christmas cantata that you really wanted? When a fellow member receives recognition and honor, do you feel a twinge of jealousy? Does your kingdom crumble when a "fairer" Snow White joins your Sunday school class and becomes a vital contributor to class discussion? If we could ever come to the conviction that we are truly family, it would change many of our attitudes about ourselves and others in the church. I know that I receive greater joy in seeing my children achieve than in my own achievements. If we are family, why is it so difficult to see another member of our own body receive honor? Our measure for evaluating our gifted self-image is not another body member, but our faithfulness in employing our unique gift for the good of the family itself.

Paul pressed home the body imagery in an unmistakable fashion:

"Now you are Christ's body, and individually members of it" (v. 27).
All the believers in Corinth were inextricably related to all other
body members. The reminder that they were individually related to
the body indicated that they were not simply absorbed into the body,
losing their own personal identity, but that each had a distinct place
and function by the grace of God. A correct understanding of spiritual gifts is one of the most affirming and challenging of all biblical
doctrines. You are important to the proper functioning of your
church. Are you presently serving according to your gift? If not,
your church is weaker for it and your image of your worth in the
kingdom of God is distorted.

The Second Gift List

In spite of all that Paul has said about each individual being gifted,
some may not have been convinced practically. After all, they could
not find their gifts among those listed in verses 8-10. It is for this
reason that Paul included a second listing of gifts which differs from
the first in several distinct ways.

Paul began with a numerical order that includes persons rather
than abilities. It is unwise to read too much into the order of the
entire list. Nevertheless, it is obvious that the numbering, plus the
use of persons, was intended to draw attention to the apostles,
prophets, and teachers. The listing of individuals would have caused
the Corinthians to think concretely of persons who were carrying out
these functions in their community. The apostles, prophets, and
teachers were involved in leadership functions.

Many of the difficulties in Corinth can be traced to the spirituals'
willingness to criticize and disregard their leaders and to press for
their own rights. Paul's apostolic authority had little meaning to the
spirituals. They judged a person by his commanding presence and
dramatic gifts (see 2 Cor. 10:10 to 12:13).

First Corinthians 16:15-16 indicates that there were persons, no-
tably the "household of Stephanas," who had emerged as leaders of
the Corinthian congregation. It seems apparent that they were being
ignored by the spirituals. Paul called the spirituals to be in subjection
to such men and to acknowledge them. In this second list, with its
emphasis on the apostles, prophets, and teachers, Paul was clearly
saying that there was a leadership structure which had been established by God and that these leaders were also gifted. The breadth of

the Pauline concept of "gifts" is becoming apparent. The abilities that enabled these men to lead are no less miraculous and no less "spiritual" than those abilities being displayed by the spirituals.

This list includes what we might call mundane service abilities. Two unusual gifts occur only in this list—"administrations" and "helps" (v. 28). To the spirituals the ability to administrate or to do helpful tasks must have seemed pretty mundane and lacking in demonstrative power. These two gifts always remind me of individuals who argue that they can't teach or sing in the choir, but that they will be glad to help keep the records or work in the parking lot. Then they sadly sigh, "I guess I'm not too gifted." There's good news if you think you fit one of those two categories! The ability to do those functions in such a way that they build up the community are gifts from God enabling you to serve, and they are just as supernatural as any other gift for ministry. These functions were deemed to be "unseemly" or "weaker" (vv. 22-23) by the "powerful" spirituals, but they had misunderstood the purpose of the gifts. Don't fall into the same trap.

We have just looked at two Pauline gift lists in one chapter. Why should he include two lists in a single chapter? The two lists are critical to Paul's broadened understanding of spiritual gifts. The first list enumerated only the prized gifts of the spirituals—the visibly "miraculous" ones. In the second list Paul literally pulled the top and the bottom out of the first list and expanded the accepted definition of spiritual gifts. He added leadership abilities and service abilities.

This should warn us when we are attempting to discover our own gifts that we need not treat Paul's gift lists as comprehensive. Neither do we gain anything by adding the two lists together and attempting to calculate the number of gifts available to the church. These lists were teaching tools, and Paul selected gifts that would illustrate the point he wanted to make.

Paul followed this second list with a series of rhetorical questions that pointedly established the demand for diversity in the body of Christ. All the questions anticipate a negative reply. Paul actually repeated the new list of gifts given in 12:28 with the omission of "helps" and "administration." Could it be that Paul left these out to draw particular attention to them? While it may be obvious that all do not have leadership roles or possess "miraculous" sign gifts, all are gifted for some form of ministry even if it may "appear" to be quite mundane. Nothing that God gives is mundane, nor should it be neglected. If you have been feeling left out when you read all the gift lists, this should provide strong encouragement to continue the search.

Desire the Greater Gifts

Upon first reading, verse 31 you might tend to be confused. "I thought that all the members were equally important. How could Paul say 'desire the greater gifts'?" It is possible that this verse may echo a slogan of the spirituals. Paul, on several occasions in this letter, quoted a slogan of the spirituals and then immediately corrected or redefined it. For example, 10:23 contains both a slogan of the spirituals and its immediate correction. "All things are lawful, but not all things are profitable. All things are lawful, but not all things edify." In each instance that Paul referred to zeal for gifts (12:31; 14:1, 12, and 39), he immediately qualified the phrase by the discussion that followed.

Paul appealed to their zeal for gifts in order to encourage them to be zealous for the greater gifts. What then is meant by "greater gifts"? It couldn't mean the ecstatic or miraculous gifts, for that would undo all that he has just said. Here once again Paul employed his favored term *charismata,* which broadened the understanding of gifts. This phrase prepares us for the full discussion of the actual use of gifts in chapter 14 and leads us to understand that the greater gifts are actually those most suited for edifying the body. This idea was implied in the emphasis on the common good in 12:7 and was further suggested by the reversal of values in vv. 21-24. While all gifts are expressions of God's grace and are necessary for the functioning of the body, some gifts are more valuable in terms of their ability to contribute to the building up of the church.

Before moving to the discussion of the edifying use of gifts in chapter 14, Paul wanted his readers, first to put the gifts in their proper perspective in the total life of the community (ch. 13). The phrase "And I show you a still more excellent way" (12:31) forces the reader to look at the bigger picture of the Christian life. Paul was not suggesting that love was a better way than gifts. Love and gifts are not in conflict, nor is love the highest of the spiritual gifts. Love is the one determining sign of true spirituality! The truly spiritual person will therefore seek gifts which enable him/her to express love and then utilize the gifts in a loving way to edify the community.

Reflections in the Mirror

1. One common Spirit, shared by all Christians, incorporates us into the body of Christ and distributes the gifts individually as He sees fit. The same Holy Spirit who gives the more public gifts, distributes the service gifts such as helps and administrations. Would you be disappointed if the Holy Spirit had chosen you for a service gift? _____ Why? _____

2. Spiritual gifts are actually grace gifts and thus tell us nothing about the possessor, but everything about the giver. Have you been guilty of judging your worth by comparing yourself to someone whom you consider to be more gifted than yourself? _____ Are you willing to trust God's Word when He tells you that He has gifted you just as He desired? _____ God doesn't make junk!

3. As in the human body, the following apply to spiritual gifts:

   a. There is only one body made up of many members brought together by one common Spirit.

   b. God gives diverse gifts in order to enable the body to function properly. The focus of gifts is on function and not on status. Lesser or weaker gifts is not in God's vocabulary.

   c. God sovereignly designed the body to include every believer. Our sole concern is to please our Creator in the use of our gifts.

   d. Since God designed the body, there are no useless appendages. How can we think ourselves to be useless if God designed us?

   e. The body demands that each part care for all other parts. If any part suffers, the whole body is affected. If one part fails to function, the body becomes less effective.

4. Where do you fit in the body of Christ? If you feel like a useless appendage, what do you think is the source of that feeling? It can't be from God. Do you think it could be a one-liner from a distorted mirror in your past? Are you willing to replace that mirror with God's perfect mirror?

5. Calling any gift "ordinary" loses sight of the fact that God always works in supernatural ways. Are you willing to accept God's Word that your gift is special and so are you?

6. One of the building blocks for self-image is a sense of empowering. Do you realize that God has empowered you to successfully serve Him by indwelling you through the Holy Spirit?

Love: The True Reflection of Spirituality

The Corinthians were facing a dilemma. If possessing certain gifts did not prove spirituality, then what sign should they seek? They knew now that all believers alike shared in the work of the Spirit in conversion, incorporation into the body of Christ, and the possession of gifts for service to the community. But was there any true reflection of one's growing spirituality? Surely the Corinthians must have been wondering: "How can we know when we're serving empowered by the Holy Spirit? Paul, do you have a mirror for that?" Perhaps these same questions have bothered you. You're welcome to listen in as Paul answers these concerns for the Corinthians.

A Word to the Wise

It's impossible to read 1 Corinthians 13 without being impressed by its beauty, style, and depth of teaching. Rarely do we attend a wedding without hearing this great hymn to love. Yet the beauty of this passage has often caused readers to ignore its context and thus to see its important corrective role in the controversy surrounding gifts in Corinth. It is not accidental that this chapter falls between Paul's broadened definition of spiritual gifts and his explanation of how gifts were to be used in the gathered assembly. This chapter is actually the peak of Paul's corrective teaching on gifts and must be fully understood before we are prepared to read chapter 14.

Nonetheless, the style of chapter 13 does differ radically from its immediate context. Why would Paul change stylistic gears right in the middle of the discussion of gifts? You might be interested to know that we find a similar style of writing in other wisdom literature of this same period. I think that Paul intentionally chose to use this style in order to meet the spirituals on their own ground. The spirituals loved to boast of their wisdom, and Paul now displayed wisdom teaching of his own. Paul had been attacked by the spirituals because his preaching lacked persuasive words of wisdom. Ironically, Paul used "persuasive words of wisdom" to express his most pointed correction. In 2 Corinthians 10—13 Paul used a similar approach to counteract the boasting in signs and visions. Paul joined his opponents in their boasting, but he boasted about his weaknesses rather than his visions and miracles.

Love, the Sign of Spiritual Maturity

Paul now moved his teaching to a higher level, virtually interrupting his discussion of gifts. He needed to do this because the spirituals linked gifts with persons as proof of spirituality. First Corinthians 13 is primarily about *persons* and only secondarily about gifts. Paul offered a comprehensive redefinition of the spiritual person. The first three verses demonstrate that Paul was concerned with the worth of persons and not just with gifts themselves. Paul was not placing love against gifts, thus making love the way which renders gifts unimportant. Who would call the work of the Spirit unimportant? Nor was he describing a way which all must walk, whether gifted or not—for *all are gifted.*

You will recall that the spirituals zealously desired miraculous sign gifts to prove that they already reigned. This chapter points to love as the one expression of the eternal which is available in the present. *Love then is the sign that one is an authentic spiritual person.* We find a clear echo of this truth in Romans 5:5; "And hope does not disappoint, because the love of God has been poured out within our hearts through the Holy Spirit who was given to us." Love is the one sure sign of the indwelling presence of the Holy Spirit whose work it is to make us over in the likeness of Christ Himself. For that reason you will find a remarkable similarity between love in this chapter and the fruit of the Spirit in Galatians 5:22-23. Both are the reflection of Christ in the life of the believer produced by the indwelling of the Holy Spirit.

The moment you receive Christ, the Holy Spirit comes to indwell you. His presence will be evidenced by His activity in your life to reproduce the image of Christ in you. Paul touched on this same theme in 2 Corinthians 3:1-18. In that passage he compared the ministry of the Spirit in the believer's heart with the work of the Ten

Commandments written on stone. Even though those Commandments clearly reflected the glory of God, they produced a ministry of condemnation in human flesh because no one was able to live up to those standards by exertion of the human will. But now as we turn to Christ and receive the Spirit there is liberty. That does not mean that we can ignore God's law; on the contrary, it means that the Holy Spirit indwells us, enabling us to obey the law. Listen to 2 Corinthians 3:18; "But we all, with unveiled face beholding as in a mirror the glory of the Lord, are being transformed into the same image from glory to glory, just as from the Lord, the Spirit."

The true sign of the Spirit's presence is the outworking of God's moral law as the image of Christ comes to be seen and experienced in our human relationships. Love is relational; it finds its authenticity in the reality of God's love experienced in Christ. It then must be lived out in the context of community. The Christian is called to walk in love. The expression of love is not an activity of the human will, but it is made possible only by the power of the Holy Spirit who indwells us. Paul emphasized this practical, visible expression of love to counteract the egotistical individualism of the spirituals. Love will be the controlling factor in the authentically spiritual person's desire for and use of spiritual gifts.

Paul's corrective is driven home with sledgehammer-like blows by comparison with the vaunted "sign-gifts" of the spirituals. He began with the prized gift of tongues and concluded that this gift exercised without love made one a noisy gong or a clanging cymbal. Tongue speech was valued because the mysterious nature of this gift made it particularly valuable as a sign of the Spirit. This gift still seems to be at the heart of much of the confusion over spiritual gifts.

Love is the mark of an authentic spiritual person.

What does Paul mean by "the tongues of men and angels?" (v. 1). Did he really believe that through tongues one communicated with the angels? Some readers have thought so, and they have looked to 1 Corinthians 14:2 and 2 Corinthians 12:4 as proof. The first passage simply asserts that men do not understand tongue speech and that, at best, it serves as a prayer language to God. The 2 Corinthians passage is more relevant. Notice, however, that what Paul heard in

Paradise was "inexpressible words, which a man is not permitted to speak." Since the revelation in the vision could not be uttered, it could not refer to tongues since that gift relies upon speech. Later in this chapter (13:10) Paul indicated that tongues would cease "when the perfect comes." If "perfect" refers to the fullness of God's kingdom in heaven, why would tongues cease just when they would prove to be particularly useful in talking with the angels face to face? No, Paul did not think that people could communicate with the angels through tongue speech.

It is, however, likely that the spirituals themselves believed that their tongues enabled them to communicate with the angels. What better evidence could one have that he already reigned? In this case 2 Corinthians 12:4 is a pointed corrective. Man is neither able nor permitted to speak what he hears in Paradise.

Paul's corrective was sharp. He used himself to present a hypothetical case reflecting the claims of the spirituals. Notice that the individual who spoke in tongues but who lacked love became like a noisy gong or clanging cymbal. Paul was not yet concerned about the edifying nature of any one gift, but he was simply describing the effect of the individual who lacked love. "Noisy" and "clanging" may allude to sounds present in pagan worship. Then he would be saying that tongues practiced by a person lacking love are much like the noisy clanging of pagan worship. Bottom line: tongues do not prove spirituality.

"Prophecy," "mysteries," and "knowledge" are closely related because they all demand special revelation in order to function. It is difficult for us to reconstruct the subtle distinctions between these gifts. The boast of the spirituals is clearly reflected in the phrase "in all speech and all knowledge" (1:5). Our attention is again drawn to the arrogant emphasis on abundance with the fourfold repetition of "all." They knew "all mysteries," had "all knowledge" and "all faith" (13:2).

A number of community problems in Corinth were related to the spirituals' claims to possess special knowledge. The most striking example occurs in chapter 8. The spirituals had freely partaken of the meat offered to idols on the basis of their knowledge. Paul's corrective was twofold. The results of their "supposed" knowledge was arrogance (v. 1) and "a stumbling block to the weak" (v. 9), whereas the outcome of love would be edification. Second, their knowledge was not full but partial (v. 2), a point which will be clarified in 13:12.

Miracle-working faith is next in this listing of gifts. It is entirely conceivable that some of the spirituals had offered miraculous deeds as evidence of their spiritual status. Second Corinthians 10—13 indicates that they were impressed with signs and wonders. In that passage Paul reluctantly entered their game of boasting, but he turned the tables by boasting about his hardships and weakness. With some hesitation, he noted that his own ministry had been accompanied by the signs of a true apostle. The Gospels make it abundantly clear that signs and wonders were clearly evidenced in Jesus' ministry. This is understandable when we remember that during the three years of Jesus' earthly ministry the spiritual battle which is normally waged in the "heavenly places" (Eph. 6:12) was conducted on an earthly stage. When the Son of God came in human flesh, Satan concentrated his evil forces on earth to do battle with the Son. Satan's ultimate defeat was sealed on the earthly stage when Jesus rose from the dead. The spiritual battlefield is once again in the heavenly places, and Satan, the conquered adversary, uses deception and accusation to wage war against the saints.

The Book of Acts makes it clear that similar "signs and wonders" accompanied the ministry of the early apostles. Paul, however, focused on the "sign" of conversion as the primary sign of apostolic ministry. In Romans 15:19 Paul mentioned "signs and wonders," and the words that follow describe his preaching. "In the power of signs and wonders, in the power of the Spirit; so that from Jerusalem and round about as far as Illyricum I have fully preached the gospel of Christ."

We have noted that many of the problems in Corinth were related to their fascination with miraculous "signs." The spirituals had attempted to regularize and congregationalize that which God intended as a sign for the establishment of the New Testament church through the ministry of the first-century apostles. For example, the Pentecost event itself was an unrepeatable sign of the outpouring of the Spirit in the inauguration of the church. There can be only one inauguration. Yet the Corinthians were fascinated with sign gifts and wanted to reproduce them in the worship service without any thought to their impact on the unbelievers and ungifted. The apostolic sign gifts, such as the raising of the dead, need not be repeatable in every generation since the apostles served for only one generation. For this reason the ministry gifts were given through the church and must be discovered and used within the context of the church in each generation to enable the church to fulfill the Great Commission. The ministry gifts will be necessary until the present order is completed by the return of the Lord. Paul again concluded this listing of "prophecy," "mysteries," "knowledge," and miracle-working "faith" by indicating that when these gifts were exercised without love; "I am nothing" (v. 2).

In verse 3 Paul was probably alluding to the spirituals' disregard for their physical bodies. Their attitude had been expressed arrogantly and destructively in acts such as incest (ch. 5) and sexual denial (ch. 7). Paul, in order to make his point strongly, took a positive expression of disregard for bodily existence. He then concluded that an act of sacrifice, even for the most noble of purposes, would be of no benefit. This would make the contrast with the selfish Corinthians even more vivid. We might paraphrase: "You disregard the physical body for selfish reasons such as sexual indulgence and you're proud of that. Even if I were to disregard my body for the most noble reason possible, to benefit others, and I lack love, it is of no spiritual benefit to me."

None of the boasts of the spirituals held up because in the important category of true spirituality—love—they came up zero.

Love Versus the Spirituals

The spirituals in Corinth were so arrogant that it was altogether possible that they would miss the point of Paul's corrective. For that reason Paul contrasted love with the actual behavior of the spirituals. He chose the eight negative statements that define what love is not to demonstrate conclusively that the spirituals lacked the one true sign of spirituality.

The two positive statements, "Love is patient, love is kind" (v. 4) are introductory. "Patient" and "kind" emphasize one's behavior in relation to others. Patience is particularly important to the proper functioning of the gifted community. Love which is patient and kind will not be jealous. The word translated "jealous" is the same word used to describe the zeal of the spirituals. Spiritual zeal can be praiseworthy, but in Corinth zeal had degenerated into jealousy and self-striving. Their zeal for various wise leaders had divided the community and proved them to be babes and not spiritual persons. They were zealous to possess spiritual gifts, but for all the wrong reasons. Zeal, untamed by love, exhibits itself in self-seeking jealousy.

As we look into the mirror of love, this is a good time for us to do a motivation check. Why are you interested in discovering your spiritual gift? Is your zeal motivated by your desire to serve the community or is there any jealous motivation that wants to gain attention or admiration? Gifts sought for the wrong reason can cause a distorted sense of self-worth.

"Love does not brag and is not arrogant." Paul had constantly rebuked the spirituals for their arrogance and boasting. The Greek word for "brag" is only found here in the New Testament, and it suggests the picture of a windbag. The spirituals had become inflated over their wisdom and oratorical ability (see 1:5). They boasted about their freedom from the law and traditions in matters of behavior and decorum. Arrogant boasting is contrary to the nature of love.

It is so easy for us to fall into the trap of spiritual pride that we can't afford to neglect this warning. We can become arrogant about how much we do for the Lord and forget that our ability to serve is but a gift of grace. Someone tells us how great we are and we swell up with pride and lose the servant spirit and the empowering. "Love does not brag and is not arrogant."

The behavior described in verses 5 and 6 are the direct result of spiritual pride. The word "unbecoming" occurs twice in 1 Corinthians (v. 5 and 7:36). In chapter 7 Paul made reference to improper behavior toward a virgin. The context indicates that Paul was referring to the danger of unseemly sexual behavior between a man and his wife to be. Apparently some of the spirituals were unduly extending the engagement period in order to boast about their spiritual ability to withstand sexual temptation. Some had overestimated their strength and had behaved in an unacceptable manner prior to marriage.

In 14:40 Paul used an adjective derived from the same Greek root to appeal for proper behavior in the worship service. Because the spirituals wanted to display their gifts to prove their spirituality, the worship service had become disorderly, and this had led to confusion and discord. Paul demanded that there be clear guidelines for control and decency. Thus the appeal for order in worship is not simply based on that which works, but it is based on the standard of love. Love does not behave unseemly and therefore the truly gifted person will desire to exercise his or her gift in an orderly manner precisely because he or she is controlled by love.

Unseemly behavior was also evident in the celebration of the Lord's Supper, where there were divisions, revelry, and a lack of concern for the poor (ch. 11). The women who insisted on praying and prophesying with their heads uncovered had disregarded tradition and thus had behaved unseemly. The possession of spiritual gifts does not elevate us above the concern for orderly community function. Love demands that we employ our gifts in such a manner that they will enhance community relations.

We can become arrogant about how much we do for the Lord and forget that our ability to serve is but a gift of grace.

Paul touched the nerve center of the Corinthian problem with the phrase, "does not seek its own." The controversy concerning the eating of meat offered to idols was selfish to the core. There were two closely related problems. Some Corinthians were buying meat in the market that had been used in pagan worship while others were participating in social events, such as a wedding, held in a pagan temple. Paul warned those who were participating in events held in pagan temples that they might become sharers in demons. But the principle to which he ultimately appealed in both cases was that of responsible behavior toward others, instead of seeking one's own rights (8:13; 10:23-33).

Paul illustrated his corrective teaching by referring to his right as an apostle to receive support from his communities. He had, however, chosen to forego this right to remove any possible hindrance to the gospel (9:12). The sentiment of 10:24 is identical to that of 13:5; "Let no one seek his own good, but that of his neighbor." The principle of love which seeks the good of the brethren is the controlling principle for the living of the Christian life and thus for the use of the gifts. Love demands that we seek gifts for ministry with others in mind. The individual who seeks gifts for ego gratification rather than the edification of the community demonstrates immaturity.

The final two phrases of verse 5 are closely related and should be taken together. "Is not provoked" is defined by "does not take into account a wrong suffered." Love is not embittered by injuries, real or supposed. It simply does not make a mental scoreboard of them. The Corinthians, however, had hauled one another before secular judges. Paul pointedly asked, "Why not rather be wronged? Why not rather be defrauded?" Then he pondered, "Is it so, that there is not among you one wise man who will be able to decide between his brethren?" (6:5). Don't miss the very pointed correction in that verse. They were arrogant about their wisdom, yet they weren't wise enough to settle simple disputes in the fellowship.

If we are interested in discovering our spiritual self-image, we cannot leave this in the Corinthian past. How often do you find yourself demanding your rights? Do you ever find yourself marking a mental scorecard? "I owe you one! I'll get you back for that." Love is so prepared to forgive that it doesn't mark the score. Do you have scorecards of unforgiveness that need to be erased so that you can clearly see the image of Christ being formed in you?

Love "does not rejoice in unrighteousness, but rejoices in the truth" (v. 6). Simply put, love finds no joy in sin! In chapter 5 we find an account of a man living with his stepmother. Paul was not only concerned about the deed, he was staggered by the reaction of the spirituals. Instead of mourning and taking disciplinary action, they had become arrogant (vv. 2-6). For this reason Paul did not simply say that love does not practice unrighteousness, but he said love "does not rejoice in unrighteousness."

Love demands that we employ our gifts in such a manner that they will enhance community relations.

Love, unlike the spirituals, rejoices in the truth. Truth here is the opposite of unrighteousness. Paul was thus asserting that love rejoices in obedient, ethical behavior. The authentic spiritual person can never be indifferent to moral considerations. Yet today we find people who want to give the appearance of spirituality, and then use it as a cover for unrighteous behavior.

We are always shocked when we hear of a pastor or televangelist who has used their position for sinful gain. Rightly so! Spiritual maturity should be evidenced in ethical behavior. But we must equally apply this principle to all believers. We are all gifted by God for ministry. We have all received the Spirit empowering us for ministry. It is always wrong when we use "claimed spirituality" as a cloak for sin. This applies to the single adult who pretends to be spiritual in order to get a date or to the business person who uses church membership to increase business. The possession of a spiritual gift does not place us above the standard of God's law. Rather the possession of God's grace expressed in our gift should make us more conscious of our responsibility to rejoice in the truth.

Having finished his contrast of love and the spirituals, Paul broke into positive acclamation about the superiority of love. Not only does love avoid the exaggerated behavior patterns of the spirituals, but love "bears all things, believes all things, hopes all things, endures all things" (v. 7).

The Eternal in the Now

You'll recall that the spirituals believed that they already possessed the fullness of the kingdom. Verses 8-13 are radical surgery on this aberrant view. In this section Paul destroyed the framework on which they arrogant spirituality had been constructed. Paul again accepted their boast of an abundance of gifts, but now his correction took a most unexpected turn. He argued that their possession of gifts actually disproved their claim to reign spiritually. Prophecy, tongues, and other gifts were earthly manifestations and thus signs, so to speak, of earthly existence. Their boasting had literally become their undoing. The possession of any spiritual gift proved beyond question that the possessor still belonged to the same earthly body as all other believers. Love, which they did not display, was the greatest expression of the eternal in the present age.

The transient nature of all spiritual gifts is made explicit in verse 8 with the repetition of "done away; . . . cease; . . . done away." Prophecy, tongues, and knowledge were mentioned here because of their prominence in Corinth, but the truth presented here holds for all gifts. All gifts are destined to pass away when the perfect comes. Obviously the gifts did not have the eternal sign value assigned to them by the spirituals.

The repetition of "in part" in verse 9 and the stark contrast between "perfect" and "partial" in verse 10 was critical to Paul's corrective. At best, the present manifestations of prophecy and knowledge were imperfect and partial. Quite a shock to the spirituals who boasted of *all knowledge*. What then did Paul mean by "the perfect?" "When the perfect comes" knowing "in part" will be replaced with face-to-face knowledge. Paul was not talking about the Christian coming to maturity, but about the perfect which would replace the partial. "The perfect" then refers to the end of this age. When Christ returns, gifts will have no value because then believers will see face to face and know as fully as they are now known by God.

Spiritual gifts do have a value, but they must be evaluated in terms of their role in the present age. They are manifestations of the *now,* and thus are limited to and by the present age. When the Lord returns ("the perfect"), there will be full participation in the kingdom, but, ironically, this will mean the demise of the gifts as they are now experienced.

The illustration of childhood should be taken at face value. Speaking, thinking, and reasoning refer to normal functions of childhood. Childish thinking and behavior are not evil, they are simply inadequate in comparison with mature speaking and thinking. The adult sets aside childish thinking because it has been surpassed by maturity. The implication is obvious! The spiritual manifestations of this age, no matter how magnificent they may seem now, will seem childish in comparison to the fullness to be experienced when the kingdom is fully realized. Paul did not want them to lay aside their gifts now. That would contradict the discussion of chapter 12. He did, however, want them to seek and view gifts in their proper perspective. They are manifestations of God's grace in the present that enable the believer to minister for the good of the body.

Spiritual gifts have meaning only when they are used for building up the body of Christ.

A second illustration presents a more pointed contrast between the nature of the gifts experienced "now" and the fullness of the coming of the kingdom. The spirituals had claimed to possess "all knowledge (1:5 and 13:2). They believed this full knowledge was evidence that they already reigned. Paul countered by asserting that present knowledge was like the dim image in a mirror, whereas the knowing when the kingdom is fully experienced will be like seeing face to face.

The mirrors of Paul's time were not as refined as ours today. The reflected image was often dim or distorted. Knowing *dimly* is not a fault. Present knowledge, by its very nature, is partial. At its very best it will be obscure when contrasted with perfect knowledge. Paul proved two things with this illustration. First, he demonstrated that possessing gifts actually proved that a person was still of this earth, for gifts have value and meaning only for service now. Second all gifts are partial and not perfect. Gifts do not possess any sign value; they possess only service value. Here, once again, we need to do a quick check in the mirror of motive. Do I desire to discover my gift for service or glory?

Paul concluded this chapter with an exclamation on the superiority of love. "But now," in contrast with the spiritual manifestations, there remain eternally faith, hope, and love. Faith or trust in the Lord begins in this life when we receive Christ, and that relationship will continue into eternity. Our conversion gives us a sure hope that will not disappoint, and in the eternal presence of the Lord that Hope will find total fulfillment. Yet even these are exceeded by love. Faith and hope focus only on our relationship, while love enables us to look outward and edify others in the present existence. Thus it is superior to faith and hope.

The claim to spirituality based on miraculous gifts is invalid because gifts are limited to earthly existence. The greatest eternal reality available in the now had been found to be conspicuously lacking in Corinth. Chapter 13 denies gifts any personal sign value, but it does not render them worthless. On the contrary, they can now be seen in the *proper perspective*. Gifts of grace are manifestations of the now, and thus their real meaning is discovered only when they are used by the "spiritual person," as defined in chapter 13, to express the eschatological reality of love in the now. More simply, spiritual gifts have meaning only when they are used for the edification of the body. With this broadened understanding of gifts and with the redefinition of the spiritual person, we are now ready to consider how we can use our gifts in the community of believers.

Reflections in the Mirror

1. The one true sign of an authentic spiritual person is the presence of love, a reflection of the indwelling Holy Spirit. Love should be the controlling factor in our desire for and use of spiritual gifts. Does your love for Christ, His church, and your fellow members in the body of Christ, motivate you to seek and use your gifts in service?

2. How do you react when you are wronged? Do you respond

with love or do you seek to get even? Do you have any mental score-boards that need to be erased? Will you take the steps to forgive and seek reconciliation in all these cases? Remember the body depends upon the harmonious working of the individual parts and your self-esteem relies on your reflection of the love of Christ.

3. The gifts of ministry were given for the edification of the body. The selfish desire for sign gifts does not reveal the unselfish desire of love. What gifts do you see demonstrated in your church that accurately reflect the love of Christ? _____ _____. Write a note of appreciation to those who minister to you through their gifts. What are you presently doing for others that reflects the love of Christ? _____

4. Since spiritual gifts will be replaced by Christ when He returns, we should seek those most effective for the edification of the church. If through our gifts, we express love through ministry, our lives can have eternal consequences. For example, when we use our gifts to lead someone to Christ, that action impacts eternity. When we use the gift of teaching to encourage others in their faith, we impact eternity. What are you presently doing that will have eternal significance? _____ What would you like to do? _____

Choosing and Using Gifts
to Reflect Love

I believe I'm beginning to get the picture. The image in the mirror is getting clearer. You're telling me that gifts don't prove anything about my spiritual worth. They don't offer a sign that I've been baptized in the Spirit or that I have arrived. They simply prove that God is gracious and will gift His church for any task it faces. I can see now that I have actually been trying to put the Holy Spirit in a box and that I've been guilty of limiting His work by not realizing that ministries such as teaching or administration require spiritual gifts. You tell me that gifts are given to edify the body and that love will concretely express itself in edifying behavior.

Well, I still have a few questions!

- What do I do now?
- Which gifts should I seek?
- Do the miraculous manifestations like tongues have any place in the assembly?
- How do we control the confusion caused by so many gifted members?
- Do you have any suggestions for our gifted women?

What's the Goal?

The question about the objective of spiritual gifts is always relevant. The goal for seeking and using gifts must correspond with God's purpose in giving the gifts. God gives the gifts to enable individual members to participate meaningfully in the life and mission of the church. Thus, we should seek gifts with that goal in mind and use them accordingly.

The first verse in 1 Corinthians 14 brings this subject to a practical conclusion. "Pursue love, yet desire earnestly spiritual gifts, but especially that you may prophesy." In chapter 12 Paul presented a radically new and broadened understanding of gifts, and in chapter 13 he redefined the spiritual person in terms of one whose life-style is characterized by love. These two insights are now brought together in a practical way in chapter 14. The relevant question is: "How would the spiritual person respond to the needs of others in seeking and utilizing the gifts?

When you read chapter 14 the word that stands out is *edification*. Paul used this word to bring the spirituals back to earth. They could use their gifts to build up the body of Christ. Ironically, such a responsible use of the gifts in the now has eternal significance. Spiritual persons can use earthly gifts to express the eternal reality of love through the body of Christ. Love expressed through the gifts is experienced in terms of edification. When love is the controlling concern of the individual, the zeal to edify will always determine the gifts we most desire and the use of those which are given. Verse 12 is the key verse in the entire chapter: "So also you, since you are zealous of spiritual gifts, seek to abound for the edification of the church." Gifts of grace provide the means whereby the spiritual person can communicate love to others.

The goal for seeking and using gifts must correspond with God's purpose in giving the gifts. God gives the gifts to enable individual members to participate meaningfully in the life and mission of the church.

Another quick check in the mirror is in order. What is your primary motivation in discovering your gift(s)? Would you be just as happy to discover that your gift is such that it enables you to serve in an unheralded support capacity?

Why Prophecy and Tongues?

When you read chapter 14 you will notice that Paul devoted a great deal of attention to prophecy and tongues, two of the most desired gifts in Corinth. There are several reasons for this. First, these were popular gifts and both were being abused by the spirituals to prove their spirituality. Thus Paul wanted to demonstrate how persons concerned about edification could use these two gifts for the common good. Second, these two gifts share a number of similarities and differences and thus provide a contrasting example by which Paul could illustrate which gifts were "the greater gifts" (12:31).

In one sense these two gifts and their proper use are discussed, but in a greater sense these two gifts are used in a representative fashion and the conclusions reached in relation to these two gifts can be applied to all gifts. When I speak on spiritual gifts, the first question I am asked always relates to tongues. When I was first interviewed about my book *Spiritual Gifts: Empowering the New Testament Church* the headlines read, "Baptist Pastor Has New Interpretation of Tongues." Oh well, it did at least create excitement about the book!

Spiritual persons can use earthly gifts to express the eternal reality of love through the body of Christ.

Tongues create the same fascination for believers today that they did for the Corinthians. Tongues have that "miraculous and mysterious" quality which creates such interest that many folks miss the real point of chapter 14 and thus of the actual purpose of gifts. Even if tongues has never been an issue or matter of interest with you, chapter 14 is still important. Paul used tongues and prophecy to illustrate the gifts most edifying for the gathered assembly, and he also discussed how confusion could be avoided when many gifted members desired to participate. Therefore, in order to understand what Paul says in chapter 14 we will deal with the question of tongues, but please don't lose track of the central argument, the use of gifts for the edification of the body.

The phrase "especially that you may prophesy" in 14:1 directs the reader's thought back to 12:31 and the emphasis on greater gifts. The greater gifts, simply stated, are those which are best suited for edifying the community. In contrast, the spirituals placed more importance on gifts that would be a sign of "spirituality." The phrase "especially that you may prophesy" established the priority of prophecy and, in a representative fashion, the priority of all intelligible and edifying gifts.

The controlling thought of the first twenty-five verses of this chapter is the intelligibility of prophecy and the corresponding unintelligibility of tongues. Thus the first reference to tongues in verse 2 must be understood in the light of Paul's overarching concern for intelligible gifts. The statement that one speaking in a tongue speaks to God is not, in the first instance, a positive affirmation concerning tongue speech, but a contrast to the prophet who speaks to people for edification. Keep in mind that Paul was establishing the priority of prophecy in terms of intelligibility.

The emphasis of verse 2 falls on the phrase "no one understands." Tongues were simply inferior when it came to the matter of edification because they could not be understood. Likewise the phrase, "in his spirit he speaks mysteries" must be understood in light of the entire context. It simply explains why no one understands tongue speech.

Gifts of grace provide the means whereby the spiritual person can communicate love to others.

In contrast, the prophet speaks to people "for edification and exhortation and consolation" (v. 3). The use of these three words strengthens the contrast between tongues and prophecy. Now having described prophecy and tongues, Paul compared the edifying value of each of these gifts: "One who speaks in a tongue edifies himself; but one who prophesies edifies the church" (v. 4). The contrast between "edifies himself" and "edifies the church" leads to the conclusion of verse 5, where Paul expressed a clear preference for prophecy.

If we read other statements in this chapter about the value of tongues (vv. 17 and 28*b*), it can hardly be denied that Paul believed that the greatest benefit of tongues was personal and not corporate. It had value for personal devotional life. Yet "edifies himself" in verse 4 was not primarily intended to establish a beneficial aspect of tongues, but to contrast it with prophecy, which edifies the church. In light of the Corinthian problems and the present context, we cannot ignore earlier injunctions such as "let no one seek his own good, but that of his neighbor" (10:24) and "love does not seek its own"

(13:5). Edifying oneself is admittedly pale in contrast to the opportunity of edifying the church. Paul's first concern was the value of these two gifts in the gathered *community* and not their value for *personal* devotions. In this context, prophecy was preferred.

The phrase, "Now I wish that you all spoke in tongues" (v. 5) was not a concession to those in Corinth who would insist on the important sign value of tongues. The emphasis is on "even more," and therefore the contrast of the preceding verse is still being advanced. Paul's wish concerning tongues cannot be taken literally as if Paul desired that everyone speak in tongues, or for that matter that everyone prophesy. Such an interpretation would contradict Paul's earlier statement that all do not speak with tongues or have the gift of prophecy (12:29-30) and would go against the emphasis on diversity in chapter 12. Paul was simply underlining the importance of seeking gifts which were better suited to edification (like prophecy) than those which were more dramatic but less edifying (like tongues).

*The greater gifts are those which are best suited
for building up the community of faith.*

The prophet was greater than the tongue speaker in terms of his ability to edify the congregation. If, however, the tongue speaker himself interpreted his speech, he, too, could edify the congregation. We can conclude that Paul expected the tongue speaker who was concerned for edification to interpret his own speech. If one possessed the gift of tongues and desired to use it for the good of the body by interpreting it, and not simply as a banner of spirituality, then he/she would be equal to the prophet. It is not that the gift of tongues plus interpretation is equal to prophecy, but that the tongue speaker who also interpreted functioned in an edifying fashion as did the prophet. You may be wondering, "Where did I get the idea that the interpreter was another person?" That's a good question and the answer seems to be tradition rather than the Bible. While the listing of interpretation separately in 12:10 would allow for interpretation to be a distinct gift, it does not demand it. If you will carefully follow the text, I think you will agree that Paul expected the tongue speaker to interpret for himself in order to edify the body.

How Then Do We Choose Gifts?

In verses 6-8 Paul used several rhetorical questions (with himself as the example) to underline the superlative value of edifying gifts. Paul first asked how he could help the Corinthians if he came speaking a tongue. Paul could help them only if he spoke intelligibly—by means of a revelation, knowledge, prophecy, or teaching. Although Paul could have won acceptance in Corinth with a display of spectacular abilities, he preferred to speak intelligibly in order to edify.

Paul's message here and in verses 18-19 is closely connected to his insistence that the spiritual person should forfeit his/her own rights for the opportunity to help others. Since tongues alone are unintelligible and do not edify, a truly spiritual person would gladly forfeit the right to a public display of tongues.

Paul used two practical illustrations to emphasize the importance of intelligibility. The first (v. 7) is that of a musical instrument played without a clear distinction of notes. Most parents have undergone the torturous weeks when their child first attempted to play a musical instrument. Dad's Sunday afternoon nap is rudely interrupted when a strange screeching and scratching erupts from the adjoining room. Startled, he leaps from his chair, expecting to find a child is in pain, only to greet the smiling face of his six-year-old who proudly proclaims that he has just taken up the violin. An instrument played with unclear notes is not dangerous, but it can be annoying. Paul's second illustration (v. 8)—the bugle—is different. If it is played without clear distinction, no one will know to prepare for battle. The results will be dangerous confusion and inactivity.

The words "So also you" (v. 9) strongly apply the preceding illustrations to the situation in Corinth. Unless one used his human tongue for intelligible communication, his speaking was as futile as speaking into the air. If it was important for lifeless instruments to produce intelligible sounds, how much more important was it for the Corinthians to use their tongues for intelligible speech?

Paul used one final illustration that perhaps anticipated an objection from the spirituals: "You can't compare our speaking in tongues with the indistinct notes of an instrument; they are the language of the angels." Paul conceded that no human language was without meaning in the proper context. Yet he insisted that even valid languages have no meaning if they are not understood. The speaker and the hearer will be like barbarians to each other. Anyone who has traveled abroad can identify with this. The unintelligible tongues, a source of pride for the spirituals, would not lead others to praise them as spiritual persons. On the contrary, persons who could not understand the tongues would regard the speakers as barbarians.

What then should we do? "So also you, since you are zealous of spiritual gifts, seek to abound for the edification of the church" (v. 12). Paul pressed home his main point by alluding to their zeal for gifts and attaching his own corrective, edification. Paul's primary desire was not to exalt prophecy as the gift *par excellence,* but to redirect the Corinthian zeal toward gifts best suited for the edification of the church. Zeal for spiritual gifts is commendable as long as gifts are properly understood as God's gracious manifestations given for the upbuilding of the body. One must always ask, "Do I desire a particular gift for selfish reasons, or do I seek to edify the church?" Paul's desire was not to extinguish their zeal, but to redirect it toward edifying behavior rather than emotional showmanship.

You may be asking yourself, *If the gifts are distributed by the Spirit as He wills, how can Paul suggest that Christians should seek gifts better suited to edification?* The fact that spiritual gifts are gifts from God does not mean that they cannot be sought. The principle is similar to the whole issue of prayer. In Matthew 6:8 Jesus told His disciples that the Father knew their needs before they asked. Yet in the same context He gave specific instructions for asking. We must remember that the sovereignty of the Giver does not negate the role of human responsibility in the asking. We can, and should, seek gifts that edify the church. We can do so with the confidence that God desires to give them in abundance.

Do Tongues Have a Place in the Assembly?

You've probably heard it said, "Anytime you find a 'therefore' in Scripture, you need to determine what it is 'there for.'" The "therefore" of verse 13 ties the next section to the principle stated in verse 12. The question is, "Do tongues have a place in the assembly? How can they be used for the edification of the body?"

In verse 5 Paul suggested that the tongues speaker could speak for edification if he would interpret. Paul now returns to that point more specifically. "Therefore let one who speaks in a tongue pray that he may interpret." The kind of prayer Paul speaks of in verse 13 was in normal language. The person prays to receive the gift of interpretation so that he might edify the church. Some object to this explanation because, in their experience, most persons speaking in tongues did not interpret their own speech. Our experience and practice should be determined by Scripture rather than allowing our experience to determine our interpretation of Scripture.

I would agree that it is highly unlikely that few, if any, tongue speakers in Corinth interpreted their own speech. For them it was the language of angels and to render it intelligible would lessen its sign value. Paul actually *commanded* the tongue speaker to pray that he might interpret. This gift, if it was to have any meaning in the assembly, must be rendered intelligible. Those who possessed the gift of tongues and desired to use it authentically should pray for the ability to interpret. Conversely, those tongue speakers who continued to exercise their gifts with no view to edification would demonstrate their lack of spiritual maturity.

One must always ask, "Do I desire a particular gift for selfish reasons, or do I seek to edify the church?" Paul's desire was not to extinguish their zeal, but to redirect it toward edifying behavior rather than emotional showmanship.

Verses 14-17 are best understood as practical instructions for the use of tongues plus interpretation in the assembly. The instructions are elementary, suggesting that Paul had not given the Corinthians any previous instructions for the use of tongues in the assembly. Verse 14 gives a straightforward appraisal of what takes place when one prays in a tongue. "For if I pray in a tongue, my spirit prays, but my mind is unfruitful." The contrast is between two states of consciousness and therefore "my spirit" refers to the human spirit which is caught up in ecstasy. The contrast, therefore, is between speaking in a rational state of consciousness and an ecstatic state of consciousness. Paul did not mean that speaking in tongues was the work of the Spirit, whereas prophecy or teaching was a rational exercise of the human mind. Nor was Paul suggesting that religious ecstasy should be avoided. Paul did, nonetheless, subordinate the ecstatic experience to the rational when the edification of the body was at stake. Paul reiterated this point in 2 Corinthians 5:13: "For if we are beside ourselves, it is for God; if we are of sound mind, it is for you." Religious ecstasy has its proper role in the Christian experience, but it is by nature more individual and personal. For that reason it is not well-suited for instruction in the assembly of believers.

We can, and should, seek gifts that edify the church. We can do so with the confidence that God desires to give them in abundance.

Religious ecstasy is experienced in different ways by different people. Some are moved by music, some through prayer, and still others by great religious art. Religious ecstasy is a genuine but highly personal experience. It is an experience which God gives us for our own edification. The results of ecstasy are such that they are not easily shared. It is like the experience you have when you tell someone about a beautiful vista encountered on your recent vacation. You tell about the scene with all the excitement you can muster, but you know by the placid look on your friend's face he's not impressed. In frustration you reply; "I guess you had to be there!" That is precisely the point of religious ecstasy. It is a personal gift of God. Its contents are not easily shared. It has its place, but it is not the focal point of the worship service.

Paul, himself, in 2 Corinthians 10—13, gave his testimony to a visionary experience. He did so only as a last resort to verify himself for the immature Corinthians who were impressed by the visionary experience of the so-called super apostles. He was reluctant to talk about his experience because it was inexpressible (2 Cor. 12:1-4). It was given him, he concluded, for his own edification. The danger of religious ecstasy occurs when we base our teaching on it. There is no room for discussion or opposition when someone says that God told him in a vision to do thus and so. The second problem is that we can become dependent on religious ecstasy. Ecstasy has an addictive quality in that it requires a larger dose to achieve the same spiritual high. This dependency can actually become idolatrous. We begin to desire and demand the spiritual high of ecstasy, and we neglect the spiritual disciplines that enable us to grow in our daily walk with the Lord.

Some Sunday mornings a particular hymn or anthem sends chills up my spine. The entire service seems to be on a higher level. I am often tempted to ask our minister of music to reduplicate the service the next week. But it won't be the same! You can't dictate the moving of the Spirit or religious ecstasy. We've all been guilty of trying to do so. We think that if we can return to that retreat center or to our home church, the feeling will be restored. If we pray long enough or sing loud enough, ecstasy will surely come. We're like Elijah of old who thought God could only speak in the fire, wind, or earthquake (1 Kings 19:12). And to think, he had just witnessed the Baal prophets on Mount Carmel who attempted to gain the attention of their god through frenzied dancing! Elijah was surprised to discover that God spoke in the voice of solitude. Ecstatic experience is the sovereign act of God, given for personal edification.

Paul did not mean that speaking in tongues was the work of the Spirit, whereas prophecy or teaching was a rational exercise of the human mind. Nor was Paul suggesting that religious ecstasy should be avoided. Paul did, nonetheless, subordinate the ecstatic experience to the rational when the edification of the body was at stake.

You should not confuse religious ecstasy with spiritual gifts. The discovery and use of gifts does not necessarily entail ecstasy. If you have been reluctant to talk about the work of the Holy Spirit, or seek to discover your gift because you feared that you would be swept up into uncontrolled ecstasy, you can relax. They are two different experiences. Each has validity in religious life, but they are distinct. Gifts are given to serve the body, while religious ecstasy is for personal enrichment. Gifts can be sought, developed, and employed, while ecstasy is a serendipitous experience from the Father.

In the ecstatic experience of tongues, Paul maintained that the mind of the individual remained unfruitful, that is, the words which the tongue speaker uttered had no rational content for the person praying. The believer who had this gift and desired to use it for the common good would first pray or sing in the tongue and then interpret the prayer by praying or singing with the mind so that he might edify all by making his message intelligible (v. 15). If one blessed in the spirit only, the ungifted person could not say "Amen" (v. 16). The *ungifted person* refers to any Christian who is unskilled in tongues and interpretation. The hearers in the early church signified their agreement with a prayer or teaching by saying "Amen." The tongue speaker might give thanks quite well in an uninterpreted tongue, but without interpretation he could not edify the congregation. Edification must be the primary concern for gathered worship.

You can't dictate the moving of the Spirit or religious ecstasy. We've all been guilty of trying to do so.

These instructions were followed by an unexpected boast from Paul which was intended as a sharp corrective for those who demanded to speak in tongues in the gathered assembly. Paul may have anticipated the objection that he was minimizing ecstatic gifts like tongues because he lacked them. Thus he thanked God that he possessed tongues in *greater abundance* than they did. This boast closely parallels his boast to a visionary experience in 2 Corinthians 10—13. Apparently the Corinthians were not aware that Paul had experienced tongues or visions.

Paul, who already possessed their highly valued spiritual manifestations, voluntarily refrained from publicly displaying them so that he might seek "the profit of the many" (10:33). Paul had sacrificed what the spirituals had considered to be a divine right for the good of the community. The effect of this confession depended on the fact that they did not know that Paul spoke in tongues. He had ministered among them for eighteen months and had not told them about his gift of tongues because he viewed it as a personal experience of ecstasy and not so much as a gift for ministry. Paul's preference when addressing the assembly of believers was for intelligible speech which could edify the whole. The contrast between five words of intelligible speech and a myriad of words in a tongue could not be more striking.

One Final Concern About Tongues

Tongues had been so central to the boast of the spirituals that Paul employed one last illustration to counteract the immature overevaluation of tongues and thus to curb their arrogant and destructive display in the assembly. In verse 20 Paul reversed the spirituals view of themselves: "Do not be children in your thinking, . . . but in your thinking be mature." In one stroke Paul attacked their understanding of themselves as mature "spirituals" and countered their claims to excel in wisdom and knowledge. They had demonstrated immature judgment by their zeal to possess the ecstatic gifts rather than the more edifying ones. This was not an evil decision, just a childish one.

If you have been reluctant to talk about the work of the Holy Spirit, or seek to discover your gift because you feared that you would be swept up into uncontrolled ecstasy, you can relax. They are two different experiences. Each has validity in religious life, but they are distinct.

My family has a tradition of buying Christmas gifts for each other. When our children were young they would select the shiniest item replete with lights, bells, and whistles. This choice was often accompanied by the innocent: "Won't Mom be surprised?" At times I attempted to intervene and suggest a more appropriate and practical gift. This was met with the objection: "Oh, Dad, that's boring!" I can only smile knowingly, because I did the same thing as a child. The affection for the showy and shiny is a part of childish enthusiasm. Paul was confronting a similar childlike enthusiasm for the spectacular and showy. The edifying gifts could look boring and practical in comparison. Are you interested in the showy or the useful?

In order to reinforce his argument that tongues had no sign value for the believer, Paul cited Isaiah 28:11-12. Paul selected this Old Testament passage because of its reference to foreign tongues. In its original context it referred to Israel being taken into captivity by another people. Paul wanted to make a single point: *tongues are not a sign for believers*. Paul balanced this negative statement on tongues as a sign by adding that prophecy is *a sign for believers*. This is the thrust of the entire chapter. Prophecy is a sign for believers because of its value for the life of the church.

Paul then offered a practical illustration to demonstrate the superior value of prophecy in the assembly. He first suggested a hypothetical situation in which the church came together and speaking in tongues occurred. The use of "all" in verses 23 and 24 was intended to give vivid impact to the illustration. Paul did mean to convey that all would be speaking at the same time. All prophesying would be as confusing as all speaking in tongues.

Gifts can be sought, developed, and employed, while ecstasy is a serendipitous experience from the Father.

The reader is shown the negative response by both the "ungifted" and the "unbeliever" to tongues spoken in the assembly. We are first reminded of the reaction to tongues by the ungifted Christian, as previously mentioned in verse 16. If the *Christian* who lacks the gift of tongues responds negatively, what will be the response of unbelievers? "Will they not say that you are mad?" (v. 23). The word "mad" provides the most striking contrast possible between the results of prophecy and tongues. The impact of the public demonstration of dramatic gifts was exactly the opposite of what the spirituals had envisioned. Paul's reluctance for the public display of tongues, even with interpretation, was the fear that outsiders would be so adversely affected by the tongue speech that they would react against Christianity. In other words, it would be antievangelistic. It is interesting that the point made here repeats the point made by reference to the musical instruments. In some instances the indistinct sound is merely unpleasant, while in others it is dangerous. Tongues are merely an unedifying noise to "ungifted" believers, but they are a stumbling block to the unsaved.

Paul was confronting a similar childlike enthusiasm for the spectacular and showy. The edifying gifts could look boring and practical in comparison. Are you interested in the showy or the useful?

Given the same situation, the response to prophecy will be positive. The order is reversed and prophecy's effect on the unbeliever is considered first. The three positive phrases, "he is convicted by all," "he is called to account by all," and "the secrets of his heart are disclosed" (vv. 23-24), are placed over against the single phrase "will they not say that you are mad?" If the effect of prophecy on the unbelievers was as beneficial as this, it would also be positive in relation to the Christian who does not possess the gift of prophecy. Because prophecy was intelligible, it would bring conviction of sin and the distinct awareness of the presence of God.

The impact of the public demonstration of dramatic gifts was exactly the opposite of what the spirituals had envisioned. Paul's reluctance for the public display of tongues, even with interpretation, was the fear that outsiders would be so adversely affected by the tongue speech that they would react against Christianity.

Once again Paul treated tongues with great reserve because of their possible negative impact. Interpretation would resolve the issue of edification of believers but would do little to solve the antievangelistic impact if tongues were spoken aloud in the assembly. It is not insignificant that Paul did not specifically mention tongues in any other letter. Apparently Paul viewed ecstatic experiences such as tongues and visions as having value for the individual, but little value for the assembled church.

How Do We Use Gifts in the Worship Service?

How then do we use our gifts in the worship service? No doubt the Corinthians must have wondered how all the gifted members could participate in worship in a meaningful way. With the question, "What is the outcome then, brethren?" (v. 15), Paul began much needed practical applications for the Corinthian worship service. This section clearly had in view the particular difficulties of Corinth, and therefore we cannot overgeneralize about the need to reduplicate this exact pattern today. The spirituals had little real interest in the worship service except that it provided a ready forum for the display of their sign gifts. Paul's primary corrective was making the gifts *serviceable* and *answerable* to the assembly of believers.

We have come full circle in Paul's presentation about spiritual gifts. The emphasis in this section is on the ministry of *each* believer and the concern for the *common good* which clearly reflects the principle established in 12:7: "But to each one is given the manifestation of the Spirit for the common good." Every individual could contribute to the worship service if his or her aim was to edify. Yet those whose goal was the arrogant display of sign gifts had no right to speak. This section is framed by a reference to edification ("Let all things be done for edification," v. 26) and a call to peace ("for God is not a God of confusion but of peace," v. 33). These twin convictions provide both the corporate and individual control for the use of gifts.

Paul first limited the tongues speakers to two or three "in turn" and that accompanied by interpretation. This passage is brief and thus we must be careful to interpret it in light of the entire chapter. The spirituals valued this gift because of its mysterious and spectacular nature and had given no thought to its use for edification. Could tongues be used for the common good?

Our understanding of the phrase, "Let one interpret" (v. 27) determines our interpretation of this passage. On first reading it may appear that Paul expected *one* individual to interpret the message of the two or three tongues speakers. Are we then to assume that a single person with the gift of interpretation could interpret anyone's speech? No New Testament text suggests that an interpreter was something of a universal translator for anyone who spoke in tongues.

We can alleviate this particular problem by translating this phrase, "let someone interpret." Tongues then were not to be used unless *someone* interpreted. In either case we are left with critical questions which must be answered. How did the tongues speaker know that someone was present who could interpret? Was the interpreter well-known to the church? Was it the same person each time? This suggestion offers little practical help.

I think that "let someone interpret" is the correct meaning, but I believe that Paul gave here a general principle which must be understood in light of his previous references to tongues plus interpretation. In his first mention of tongues plus interpretation, Paul's basic line of thought was that the speaker himself would interpret. In 14:13 he commanded the tongue speaker who was zealous to edify the church to pray for the gift of interpretation. The ability to interpret would enable the tongues speaker to edify the believers and avoid the risk of offending the non-Christians. In the light of these two previous texts, the suggestion that someone else would interpret seems unlikely or, at best, a rare exception. This resolves the problem of knowing when an interpreter was present. The tongue speaker could speak with confidence because he would be the "someone" who interpreted the message to make it edifying.

This means that the tongues speaker who was not an interpreter should remain silent in the church. Paul's prohibitions in this section were not aimed at keeping anyone from contributing to the edification of the assembly, they were directed at the spiritual who was seeking to arrogantly display a sign gift. Even he/she had the freedom to speak to God (14:2) and to himself (v. 4). He could practice his gift at home or perhaps silently in a moment of meditation during the worship service.

Interpretation of tongues certainly resolves the problem of the "ungifted" being able to say "Amen" (v. 16) to the message, but we are still left with the effect of tongues on the unbeliever. If we take Paul's directions in verse 15 at face value, we might further suggest that Paul anticipated that the tongues speaker would receive his message as he prayed silently in the spirit and then deliver his interpreted message audibly through rational speech. I believe this is the obvious implication of this verse, followed by the warning of verse 23 and fortified by Paul's own example (v. 19). The risk of offending the unbelievers would lead the mature Christian to forfeit the right to speak audibly in tongues. Delivering the edifying message is the goal, not revealing how one received the message.

I have had people object to this interpretation based on current practice in charismatic fellowships. We cannot allow tradition, Baptist, charismatic, or otherwise, to determine our interpretation of Scripture. Others object that this does not give the tongue speaker full freedom to practice his/her gift. No one in the church has absolute freedom to practice any gift. The prophets, too, face restrictions. Our freedom must be understood in the lordship of Christ as revealed in the community of believers. The mature believer will gladly forfeit the right to speak in order to edify the body (cf. 10:23-24) and win the lost (9:19). The mere possession of a gift does not grant one a divine right to exercise that gift without due consideration for the body of believers.

Can the tongue speaker tell the congregation that the message was received while praying in tongues? We must ask, what would be the purpose of such a statement? Does it edify the church or draw attention to the speaker and the gift possessed? Gifts have one purpose and one value when used in the assembly—the common good. I can see no way that such a statement serves the common good given the controversy that surrounds this gift then and now.

Let me illustrate this point. Suppose each Sunday I began my sermon with a detailed description of my preparation. "This week I spent eight hours in prayer and another ten hours researching and writing this message. I read five commentaries and worked through this passage in the original Greek. Here's the message God gave me for the church." Would this help you hear God's message, or would your attention be drawn to the messenger? Anything that draws attention to the speaker and away from the message is irrelevant and must be discarded as spiritual egotism.

Paul's treatment of prophecy indicates that his concept of prophecy differed substantially from that of the spirituals. Prophecy too had been abused and therefore Paul limited the number of prophetic utterances at any one service to two or three. The implicit suggestion was that a prophet could exercise volitional control over the use of his or her gift and thus it might be necessary for a prophet to leave without having an opportunity to speak.

Once a prophet had spoken, the other prophets who were not among the two or three who had opportunity to speak, could pass judgment. In controlling the prophets, why did Paul instruct the first prophet to be silent when interrupted by a second speaker? This regulation is surprising to the modern-day reader. Most of us were raised with the injunction that you don't interrupt when someone else is speaking. The interruption of the second prophet provided control for a prophet who failed to exercise self-restraint. The Holy Spirit, through the interruption of the second prophet, judged that the first prophet was speaking without inspiration.

Two elements of control should always be at work in the assembly. The mature spiritual person will, for the sake of order and the good of the whole, volitionally control the impulse to speak. If, however, he fails to do so, divine control can be exercised by others who have the authority to silence the speaker. I suspect that this regulation was directed at the spirituals who wanted only to exhibit their gifts, not to edify the body.

Our church has a special Thanksgiving Day service where we place microphones throughout the church and invite people to give a short testimony of thanks. Generally, the service moves along without a hitch. Often a deep moving of the Spirit takes place as persons testify to the working of God in their lives. Occasionally, however, we have someone who continues on after the original word of thanks. He may lecture the church concerning some failing or draw attention to his own ministry. From the vantage point of the pulpit I can see the uneasiness that develops when the speaker exceeded the moment of inspiration. At times I have had to intervene and say, "Thank you, we must allow someone else to share now." This is not unlike the regulation being placed on the prophets.

The phrase "the spirits of prophets are subject to prophets" (v. 32) has been variously interpreted and therefore dogmatism about one's interpretation is unwarranted. In the context it seems to mean that the prophets can themselves exercise volitional control. They don't have to speak simply because they feel inspired to do so. Volitional control would be necessary for the prophet to obey the regulations concerning the number of speakers and the demand for orderly sequence.

This section on orderly worship was sealed by an appeal to the very nature of God. "God is not a God of confusion but of peace." The proper use of spiritual gifts will always bear witness to the presence of God (v. 25) and the nature of God (v. 33).

People who object that they cannot control their urge to speak or burst forth in tongues or prophecy will find no encouragement from this passage. First, God places the gift under the rational control of the believer. If however, the individual fails to exercise proper control that permits an orderly and edifying assembly, others may call upon him to be silent. The possession of gifts does not elevate the possessor above the order for the church established by God.

Do You Have a Word for Gifted Women?

The third group of persons who are called to silence are certain women in the church. Paul had already addressed the issue of women participating in the worship service in 11:2-16. In that passage he granted permission for the women to pray and prophesy if they conformed to the custom held by all the churches concerning the covering of their heads. If, however, a woman chose to be contentious, "we have no other practice, nor have the churches of God" (v. 16).

Can we reconcile the approval of 11:5 with the prohibition of 14:34? Several suggestions have been put forward. 1) Paul was prohibiting women from speaking in tongues. Such an interpretation would have to be read into the text since the immediate context was prophecy not tongues. 2) Paul was prohibiting the women from judging and questioning the prophets. This would, it is suggested, require a woman to usurp or challenge the authority of a male prophet. This interpretation does take more seriously the context, but does not fully resolve the problems. Could a woman respond to the prophecy of another woman? Remember, Paul has already acknowledged their right to prophesy (11:5).

I believe a better solution to this problem can be found by paying close attention to both the historical and textual context. Remember that the command to keep silent was repeated three times. Both the tongue speaker who could not interpret and the prophet who was interrupted were required to be silent. I have suggested that in both instances Paul was concerned with silencing the spirituals who had no concern for the edification of the church. In the same manner, "Let the women keep silent in the churches" had in view the silencing of female spirituals who desired to speak in the service without regard to traditions of the church or the edification of others. Their only desire was to display their freedom.

In the case of the women, the exception which allowed women to speak in the assembly is carried over from chapter 11. Rather than repeating the complex instructions previously given, Paul introduced this section with the phrase "as in all the churches of the saints" (14:33). That phrase calls to mind the final statement of the previous discussion: "We have no other practice, nor have the churches of God" (11:16). Remember, the verse divisions were not in the original text. The phrase, "as in all the churches of the saints," makes better sense when viewed as an introduction to the issue of women speaking rather than as a conclusion to the former discussion.

Paul here brings the discussion of gifts and propriety in worship under the control of the practice in other churches. The spirituals in Corinth tended to act as if Christianity originated with them. They believed they could behave as they pleased without attention to the larger Christian community. Thus Paul asked; "Was it from you that the word of God first went forth? Or has it come to you only?" (14:36)

The contentious behavior that Paul had in mind was that of the women who demanded their right to prophesy without any regard for tradition or order. Thus Paul did not intend to rescind the permission granted in chapter 11, he desired only to silence the women spirituals who behaved shamefully. They had thrown off all restrictions of decency and order under the banner of freedom because their desire was to prove their spiritual superiority. They, like the tongues speaker who could not interpret and the prophet who was interrupted, must be silent in the church.

"Let the women keep silent in the churches" had in view the silencing of female spirituals who desired to speak in the service without regard to traditions of the church or the edification of others. Their only desire was to display their freedom.

The actual situation in chapter 11 is difficult to reconstruct because of the uncertainty about head coverings in the time of Jesus. Most likely the issue related to the styling of one's hair to be worn as a covering for the head. A Jewish woman would wear her hair tightly braided on top of her head as a covering. When a woman let her hair down in public, she was making a sexual statement. I often tell people that this section reminds me of the words of the country song that declares that when she lets her hair hang down it's behind closed doors. Remember the reaction of the Pharisees when the woman wiped Jesus' feet with her hair? "If this man were a prophet He would know who and what sort of person this woman is who is touching Him, that she is a sinner" (Luke 7:39). Her unfettered hair branded her as a harlot.

Let's attempt to reconstruct the scene. The early Jewish Christians must have had considerable difficulty when women were allowed to come into the worship service with the men. In the temple, women had been relegated to the court of women, while in the synagogue they stood outside. Worshiping together had been difficult enough and now you tell me that they have the right to pray and prophesy! The Jewish man might respond thus: "I need time to digest this new idea! Just when I've finally accepted these new truths, the women beside me stands to prophesy. She dramatically pulls the combs from her unshorn hair and it falls across my lap. Culture shock is one thing—this is too much!"

Our fictional female prophet brought dishonor to her head. We find a play on the word "head." She disgraced her own head by wearing her hair like a prostitute. If she wanted to behave like a harlot, she should have had her head shaved, the punishment for an adulteress (11:6). But her dramatic action also brought dishonor upon her husband (also her head). By releasing her hair, she had declared herself sexually available and thus had disgraced him. It was therefore fitting that in 14:34-35, when Paul reminded them of this particular occasion, he subjected the woman to her husband's authority. She had dishonored him and now she must be subjected to him.

Admittedly, both passages are difficult and you may find this reconstruction overly subtle. In any case, we must acknowledge that Paul permitted women to pray and prophesy when done properly. Yet, under certain conditions women must keep silent (v. 34). I think the solution is found in the attitude problem of the spirituals, male and female alike, who desired only to flaunt their gifts and thus prove their spirituality.

These Are the Lord's Commands

The concluding verses of chapter 14 serve as a summary statement and show the seriousness with which these corrections must be taken. Verse 36 is an ironic reference to the extravagant behavior of the spirituals who were acting as if the gospel had originated with them or that they alone were Christians. This individualistic behavior had led to confusion in worship as well as in everyday affairs. Paul reminded them that in the exercise of their gifts they must not only be mindful of the people in their own fellowship, but those in the broader Christian community.

Paul was aware that some might have been tempted to refute his teaching as one man's opinion, and one who, in their thinking, lacked miraculous sign gifts. Therefore, he left no opportunity for counterattack and no option for disobedience. "If anyone thinks he is a prophet or spiritual, let him recognize that the things which I write to you are the Lord's commandment" (v. 37). This verse has a barb to it. The spirituals entertained no doubt about their elevated status, but Paul attacked the very heart of their claims and established a new criterion for proving oneself to be a spiritual person. All who accepted the conditions of this teaching would show themselves to be spiritual. Thus we are brought once again to the two criteria which have been used throughout this letter: 1) Discernment of the graciousness of all Christian existence, and 2) behavior characterized by love.

Discovering our spiritual gifts should not produce in us arrogance but humility. It will not release us from responsible behavior in community, but will tie us more closely to community. The recognition of the grace God has given is always a humbling experience. The understanding of the gifted body reminds us of our interdependence and will cause us to guard our relationships in the body.

Don't underplay the severity of verse 35. We began this section with Paul's statement that he did not want them to be ignorant concerning the spiritual gifts (12:1). Now that they had been fully informed about their breadth and their given purpose, if the spirituals chose to ignore this teaching and use their gifts in a destructive and arrogant fashion, they would not be recognized by God. That is, they would prove themselves to be spiritual impostors. Do you see now why Paul could so boldly prohibit some from speaking in the assembly?

Paul concluded with a brief but positive summary: "Therefore, my brethren, desire earnestly to prophesy, and do not forbid to speak in tongues" (v. 39). The contrast between Paul's enthusiasm for prophecy and his provisional acceptance of tongues relates to his desire for believers to seek gifts with the edification of the body in mind. Whatever gift one possesses, one thing is certain: "But let all things be done properly and in an orderly manner" (v. 40). Is the reflection in the mirror becoming clearer? Do you see why you should desire the more edifying gifts?

Paul was aware that some might have been tempted to refute his teaching as one man's opinion, and one who, in their thinking, lacked miraculous sign gifts. Therefore, he left no opportunity for counterattack and no option for disobedience.

Reflections in the Mirror

1. Paul's primary concern in chapter 14 of 1 Corinthians was to move the zealous Corinthians to seek gifts which were most edifying

to the body. He compared tongues and prophecy in order to illustrate the priority of intelligible gifts over ecstatic ones in the context of the assembly. Ecstatic religious experiences, such as tongues or visions may be valid in and of themselves, but they do not contribute easily or well to the worship experience of the gathered church.

2. The use of tongues in worship creates two different problems. The *"ungifted" Christian* (that is, the Christian who does not have the gift of tongues) is not edified and thus cannot say the "Amen" (v. 16). The unbeliever is confused and therefore may conclude that Christians are mad. If the tongue speaker interprets his/her speech, the first problem can be overcome. The second, however, remains if tongues are spoken aloud. For this reason Paul anticipated that the mature Christian, concerned for edification, would waive the right to speak audibly in a tongue. He could share the interpreted message and thus edify the Christian and remove the antievangelistic dilemma created by spoken tongues.

3. All gifts can be controlled both by the possessor and by the community. Spiritual maturity and the accompanying desire to edify the church should cause the gifted person to waive the right to speak. If this personal control fails, the church family itself can bring control. Gifts do not elevate anyone above control. Gifts are given for edification and not personal glorification and must be employed or controlled with this in mind.

4. Because of the particular needs of the Corinthian community, Paul here dealt with gifts that would be prominent in the worship service. Therefore, he did not attempt to list all possible gifts. Many gifts, such as showing mercy, helps, and administrations are not oriented to use in the worship service. Nonetheless, all gifts must be used under the authority of the church with edification as the goal.

5. Do you desire to abound for the edification of the church? Which gifts are most needed in your church? _____ What ministries are undone or are understaffed? _____ _____ Could God be speaking to you about a gift that would enable you to serve in this particular area? Are you willing to accept His choice of gifts even if it is not what you expected?

A Highly Polished Mirror

Mirrors come in many different grades and qualities. Ancient mirrors were often made of highly polished metal. The glass mirror was a major advancement. The image in glass was much clearer and more accurate. We have looked at two different passages in the attempt to discover our true identity through our gifts. In 1 Thessalonians we discovered a very early and incomplete look at the working of the gifts. The study of that passage provided some valuable clues, particularly about the context of community, but it could not provide the polished mirror image we need. In 1 Corinthians we had to escape from the fun house of distorted mirror images before we could really begin to look into the mirror for a glimpse at an accurate reflection of gifts.

In order to discover the essential elements in Paul's teaching concerning spiritual gifts, it would be nice to have a highly polished mirror. If we could find a community that Paul had not visited and thus had not given previous instruction about gifts, it would be really helpful. Further, it would be beneficial to have a community not embroiled in controversy concerning the nature and use of the gifts. In such a situation we might obtain a clear reflection of Paul's essential teaching on gifts. The Book of Romans provides us with such a situation and with a highly polished and accurate mirror image.

Paul wrote Romans after 1 Corinthians, probably from Corinth during the three-month period described in Acts 20:3. Several interrelated concerns prompted Paul to write this letter. Paul indicated his desire to come to Rome to encourage the Christians there (1:10-15) and to solicit their support for the expansion of the gospel into Spain (15:22-29). This helps us to understand Paul's detailed theological teaching in Romans 1—11. That section reads almost like a systematic theology. If you were a missionary and wanted to gain the support of a church for your ministry, you, too, would give a clear statement of your theological position.

Yet Paul's desire to obtain support for his missionary work does not fully explain the specific admonitions in chapters 12—15. Paul's treatment of the "weak" and the "strong" indicates that he knew something about the local situation even though he had not personally been to Rome. Paul knew several members of the Roman community as Romans 16 makes abundantly clear. He must have met many of these persons during his missionary travels. We know, for example, that he lived with Aquila and Priscilla while in Corinth. No doubt Paul gathered fairly detailed information about the needs of the church in Rome from these ministry colleagues.

If we grant that Paul had some knowledge of the Roman community, we must ask whether this church was also struggling with misunderstandings about gifts. I think that we can answer this in the negative for at least three reasons. 1) The tone of the letter does not indicate any misunderstanding like that of Corinth. 2) The brevity of the gift passage would be surprising if there were problems. 3) The content of the passage is more in the form of general principles than corrective teaching. Thus this passage is somewhat of a neutral gift passage and can serve as the highly polished mirror we need. We will discover here truths concerning spiritual gifts which Paul believed to be of benefit in any situation. We will look at six principles of giftedness which will enable us to begin to get a clearer image of our own unique giftedness.

Principle 1:
The Renewed Mind

The division between theological teaching and application is more pronounced in Romans than in most of the other Pauline letters. Chapters 1—11 are basically theological in content, whereas chapters 12—15 are practical and ethical teaching. While the break is obvious, the teaching material is based on the theological truths in chapters 1—11. The two sections are linked together by the phrase, "I urge you therefore, brethren, by the mercies of God" (12:1). The instructions of chapters 12—15 are based on the truth that the hearers had received the mercies of God which were described in the first section of Romans.

The presentation of the body as a living sacrifice and the transformation by the renewing of the mind are the foundational pillars upon which the following exhortation is constructed. This once again reminds us that the foundation for the discussion of gifts is the experience of God's grace in personal relationship. For this reason we again note that the discussion of gifts is surrounded by ethical instruction which demands edifying relationships in the community of faith. Chapter 12:9-21 has many parallels with the teaching in 1 Corinthians 13. Gifts find their purpose, control, and meaning in community. If you are seeking spiritual identity through the discovery of your gift without due concern for community, your search will be futile.

Paul began this teaching section with the command: "Present your bodies, . . . to God" (v. 1). "Present" means "to place at one's disposal." The language of sacrifice reminds us of the sacrificial system of the Old Testament. But in contrast to dead animal sacrifices, we must present our bodies to God as *living* sacrifices. If we are going to feel the full impact of this passage, we must accept the fact that God wants our physical bodies. Believe it or not, that physical body you stare at in the mirror each morning is what God uses to house His precious gifts for ministry.

The foundation for the discussion of gifts is the experience of God's grace in personal relationship.

The three words which qualify "body" are of equal value. The Christian's body can be offered as a living sacrifice only because the believer has been granted newness of life through a person relationship to Christ Jesus. In Romans 6 Paul gave a full explanation of how the Christian is made alive in Christ. We are buried with Him through baptism into death so we might walk in newness of life. Before individuals accept Christ as Savior they are spiritually dead and, therefore, have nothing of value to offer God. Dead persons can't serve a living God. By God's grace our sins can be forgiven and we can be made spiritually alive. In light of this transformation we are no longer to allow sin to reign in our physical bodies, nor are we to present the members of our bodies as instruments of unrighteousness. Instead, we are to present ourselves to God as those alive from the dead and the members of our bodies as instruments of righteousness to God.

Spiritual gifts are the God-given means whereby we may serve God through our physical bodies. All the spiritual gifts operate in the context of our physical bodies, and without the gifts we would have nothing to offer back to God in service. The body as a living sacrifice must continually be presented to God in selfless service. The greatest dilemma with the living sacrifice is that it often attempts to wiggle off the altar when the coals heat up. Our service is not at our own convenience, but as living sacrifice. Our service is not really a matter of volunteerism, but it is an obligation we owe to the Lord who has given life to our mortal bodies. The whole point of spiritual gifts is that we have been gifted to serve God. We were saved for this purpose. Many Christians fail to discover their spiritual gifts because they want to choose their place and time of service. By granting us a special gift of grace God Himself has chosen our place of service (cf. 1 Cor. 12:18). Are you willing to be a living sacrifice in the place of God's choosing, or are you seeking some particular gift with your own ego in mind?

"Holy" underlines both the totality of the sacrifice and its ethical character. The Christian's body is placed at God's disposal, and the Christian who is sacrificed no longer lays claim to himself or herself. We can't ignore the needs of the body of Christ with the excuse, "My time is precious to me." We place ourselves at God's disposal. The sacrifice is "holy" in an ethical sense corresponding to the nature of God. Christians are called to holy living which requires purity in mind and body.

The body as a living sacrifice must continually be presented to God in selfless service. The greatest dilemma with the living sacrifice is that it often attempts to wiggle off the altar when the coals heat up.

This living and holy sacrifice is that which is acceptable, in the sense that it is what God requires and only that which he will accept. Anything less is inadequate. Isn't it exciting to know that through your gifts you have something to contribute which is pleasing and acceptable to the Sovereign God of the universe? That truth, in and of itself, should greatly enhance our self-image.

Remember the seven building blocks for a sense of self worth? Notice how they're related to this truth that through our gifts we make a contribution that pleases God. Doesn't that give you a sense of inherent worth, security, purpose, empowerment, and personal competence? What about building your self-concept? You're pleasing to God! What about a sense of belonging? You're part of God's plan!

The offering of ourselves is our "reasonable" act of worship in the sense that it is appropriate to the nature of Christian existence as described in the earlier chapters of this letter. Paul expressed the same idea in 1 Corinthians 6:20, "For you have been bought with a price: therefore glorify God in your body." If God has made our bodies as alive from the dead through the gift of His Son, what else other than our bodies could we give Him as an appropriate act of worship? The discussion of the use of gifts in the community is the practical outworking of appropriate Christian worship.

Through your gifts you have something to contribute which is pleasing and acceptable to the Sovereign God of the universe.

Although Christian worship takes place in a real-world situation, the Christian cannot be conformed to the values of the present age. The mind-set of this world tells us that true self-identity is found in living for oneself. The world may tell us that our true value is found in physical looks, financial attainment, or trophies and awards. It's easy to buy into these false values unless we are constantly being transformed by the renewing of our minds. "Mind" (v. 2) denotes the inner part of the constitution where feeling, thinking, and willing take place. It is not a matter of becoming more intelligent, but of the reorientation of thought and life to align with the truth experienced in Christ.

We've all been told that our thinking impacts our behavior. The pole vaulter who looks down the runway and concludes that he will never clear the bar has defeated himself before he ever plants the pole. We must, however, be careful that we don't fall into the deception of "positive thinking." Many of the popular image-bolstering books of our day are built on "positive thinking" with its promise that what your mind can conceive you can achieve. While "positive thinking" has an element of biblical truth, it also contains flawed thinking. It is accurate in its appraisal that thinking affects behavior and accomplishment. It is wrong in promising that we can achieve that which we think.

One of my favorite childhood books was *The Little Train That Could*. It was the story of a little engine that was faced with the seemingly impossible task of pulling a heavy load over a high mountain. The little train's huffing and puffing was translated into the repeated phrase; "I think I can, I think I can, I think I can." Did that inner confidence pull the train over the mountain? No, the truth of the matter is that if the little train did not have sufficient horsepower to climb the mountain, all the positive thinking in the world would not enable him to accomplish the task. Positive thinking may help us to tap our unused potential, but it will not provide additional resources. The indwelling Holy Spirit can indeed provide the supernatural resources that you need to do the seemingly impossible task.

The "renewing of the mind" enables us to see ourselves from God's vantage point. It empowers us to "prove" the will of God. "Prove" means the ability to discern and the power to embrace and accomplish the will of God in concrete activity. The biblical assertion *you can* is based on the promise of God, not positive thinking. "You may prove what the will of God is, which is good and acceptable and perfect" (v. 2). You have gifts that enable you to offer to God a pleasing and perfect offering. Is your newly reflected image looking any better? If you are pleasing to your Maker, what else do you require to be pleasing to yourself?

Principle 2:
All Are Gifted

This passage is built upon the assumption that every believer is gifted for service. Verse 6 is the key: "And since we have gifts that differ according to the grace given to us, let each exercise them accordingly." Throughout his writings Paul hammers away at the suggestion that only a few spiritually elite are gifted. If you are going to develop the proper self-identity you must believe this truth and begin to act upon it. You are gifted!

This means of course that you were not intended to be a spectator in the family of God. You were uniquely created by God and gifted for a special role by Him that will enable you to impact eternity. That thought alone ought to give you a renewed sense of self-confidence. No trick mirrors here! No distorted reflections, but an image based on the integrity of God's Word.

You may be saying, "I hear what you're saying, but I just can't find myself on any of these gift lists." That's OK! The lists were never intended to be comprehensive, but only illustrative of the sort of abilities God might give you to enable you to have a purposeful role in the fellowship of believers. Notice, for example, that the list in verses 6-8 is intentionally broad and includes gifts not mentioned in 1 Corinthians. It also omits many of the gifts listed in that letter. If Paul were attempting to give a complete listing of all the spiritual gifts, he would certainly have collected them in one place for us.

If you are pleasing to your Maker, what else do you require to be pleasing to yourself?

Look at the uniqueness of this particular list. We find gifts you might have been expecting such as prophecy and teaching. Service, leading, and exhorting are new, but not all that surprising. Giving and showing mercy, however, are unexpected. While these may sound like unusual spiritual gifts, they demonstrate the breadth of Paul's teaching about what sort of abilities might be properly classified as gifts enabling us to serve the body of Christ.

"He who gives with liberality" (v. 8) refers to the compassionate sharing of one's possessions for the benefit of others. Unfortunately, I have not found too many people who are zealous for this gift. On one occasion when I was preaching on this text, I had a young wife come to me with a huge smile on her face. "That explains it," she exclaimed. She then proceeded to tell me about her husband's passion to give. The ability and opportunity to give made him come alive and gave purpose to his labor. All of us are called to be good stewards in our giving and to minister to the needy, but some have a unique gift for giving with liberality.

Showing mercy has in mind such functions as tending the sick, relieving the poor, or caring for the aged and disabled. Notice that these benevolent tasks must be accompanied with the attitude of cheerfulness. When showing mercy is one's gift, functioning in this fashion is not a duty and thus the individual does not exhibit a spirit of drudgery. The attitude of cheerfulness will enable the recipient of the merciful act to respond positively.

Did you notice that this list lacks the enthusiastic or miraculous gifts? The gifts here fall into the two broad categories of service gifts and leadership gifts. We are reminded that Paul's discussion in 1 Corinthians 14 showed a preference for the more edifying gifts rather than the dramatic gifts when it came to the edification of the body.

If you are going to develop the proper self-identity you must believe this truth and begin to act upon it: You are gifted!

The freedom with which Paul could refer to persons or abilities is clearly evidenced again in this list. Remember that in 1 Corinthians 12:28-30 Paul began with persons (apostles and prophets) and moved to abilities (miracles and healings). Here in Romans he began with abilities and moved to persons. In other words, Paul felt the complete freedom to speak of prophets in one list and prophecy in another. It is not that the person is the gift, but the relationship between the individual and the gift possessed was so integral that an individual could be referred to in terms of the gift they possessed. If you have the gift of teaching, it is quite appropriate to refer to you as "he who teaches" (v. 7).

Why is this list so unusually broad? It served to illustrate the broad spectrum of abilities where people might discover their unique giftedness. Don't despair if you've had trouble finding yourself on a gift list. I've got some good news for you. The lists were not intended to be comprehensive, only representative.

Principle 3:
Gift Discovery Requires Sober Evaluation

As we have seen in 1 Corinthians one of the problems inherent in spiritual gifts is pride. When we see our gift as a sign of our spiritual maturity or importance in the body of Christ it can lead to destructive behavior which hurts the church.

I played linebacker on the Wake Forest football team. I was assigned certain specific responsibilities. If the offensive lineman came directly at me, I was to meet him in the line looking for a running play. If he pulled back to pass block, I retreated to a short passing zone. However, if he pulled down the line, I was to back out and mirror him expecting an end run. When a big guard pulled down the line, I was always tempted to dart through the hole created by his departure. I felt sure that I could do damage in the backfield before anyone noticed my presence. In one particular game, I succumbed to the temptation. My plan worked to perfection. I was making tackle after tackle in the opponent's backfield. At halftime we were leading the game and I was having a field day, playing everyone's position but my own. To the average fan I must have looked like an all-star.

One little catch! The opposing coaches must have seen this arrogant showboat trying to do it all. By my foolhardy attempt to play everyone else's position, I had neglected my own position and had put my team at jeopardy. Throughout the second half our opponent successfully ran a counter play that took advantage of a silly linebacker who was out of position.

When people in the church think more highly of themselves than they ought to think, they will always impact the church's ability to successfully fulfill its mission. Arrogant overevaluation is a distorted mirror image. Remember our gifts are "grace gifts" and offer no basis for boasting. Gifts tell us nothing about the possessor and everything about the giver. All are gifted and equally important to the proper functioning of the body.

A second and equally devastating problem is underevaluation. I call this the Eeyore syndrome. If you read the popular Winnie the Pooh books you will remember the little flop-eared donkey Eeyore. He slumped around with his head between his legs thinking that he was of no particular value. Individuals who claim they have no particular gift or ability may sound piously humble, but they are behaving in a way that is unbiblical and hurts the body of Christ. Take God's Word for it—*You are gifted!*

A sober evaluation of our gifted self-image is based on the promise that God has allotted to each a measure of faith. The emphasis is on the individuality of the giving of a measure of faith and not on the quantity. If it were quantity, someone might be tempted to argue that it takes more faith to exercise the gift of prophecy than the gift of service. This could lead to spiritual arrogance which is contrary to the nature of grace gifts. Or one prophet might claim that his prophetic gift was more powerful than that of a fellow prophet because of his greater quantity of faith. Both ideas are distorted and miss the point.

The entire process can be explained as follows: the prophet soberly evaluates himself and becomes aware of his gift, its nature, purpose, and limitations. He can now fully employ his gift with the singular desire to serve the good of the community. He recognizes he is but one member of the body and thus depends on the proper functioning of all other members. When you soberly evaluate yourself based on the assurance that God has given you a measure of faith, you will discover your appropriate place in the body. Thus the phrase "measure of faith" functions here in much the same way that the phrase *grace gift* does in other gift passages.

Individuals who claim they have no particular gift or ability may sound piously humble, but they are behaving in a way that is unbiblical and hurts the body of Christ. Take God's Word for it—You are gifted!

The renewed mind enables the believer to prove the will of God in relationship to his or her giftedness. This involves the twin aspects of ability to discern your giftedness and the ability to properly utilize your gift for the good of the body. Such knowing will enable you to come to a proper understanding of the nature, goal, and boundaries of your spiritual gift. The renewed mind enables us to see that our gifts are the expression of God's individualized grace and therefore it keeps us from overevaluating ourselves and becoming arrogant or from underevaluating ourselves and becoming useless.

Principle 4:
Gifts Create Unity in Diversity

In a manner reminiscent of 1 Corinthians Paul used the picture of the human body to illustrate the proper functioning of the church. The human body is a unified whole precisely because it is made up of numerous members, each with a unique function. Each member of the body has a specific role, and therefore all are equally necessary. No one member can fail to function if the body is to fulfill its God-given tasks. No one member, no matter how powerful, can fulfill all the functions of the body.

Even though the world around us clearly illustrates this principle of unity in diversity, we still struggle to believe it applies to us specifically and to our church. We watch any successful sports team and see players with unique and differing roles. If all the players wanted to play the same position or had the same skills, the team would be ineffective. Those players whose roles often seems insignificant are equally vital.

The renewed mind keeps us from overevaluating ourselves and becoming arrogant or from underevaluating ourselves and becoming useless.

When I lived in England, I decided to row crew. Our boat had eight oarsmen and a coxswain. The task of the oarsmen is pretty obvious, but I often doubted the value of the cox. He sat comfortably in the rear of the boat, never breaking a sweat. All he did was guide the boat and shout orders to the oarsmen who were doing all the work. I often wondered why we needed him at all. If we could dump this turkey it would lighten our load and make our task easier.

The races in the narrow and winding Cam River were called the "bumps" because the object of the race was to physically bump the boat in front of you before the boat behind you bumped you. Since all the oarsmen are looking backwards, the only one who can see the boat in front of you is the cox. The team devises signals that can be sent in by the bank party that follows the boat, usually by riding a bike along a foot path on the shore. The signals work well in practice, but on the day of the race, they are lost in the cacophonous noise created by the crowd and the bank parties from the other boats.

The races last four days and the objective is to get four consecutive bumps. We had achieved our goal the first two days and were looking good. On the third day we quickly pulled up on the boat in front of us. We were leaning heavily on the oars in a concerted effort to make our third bump when we felt the shock and heard the grating sound that seemed to assure victory. To our horror we looked around only to see that our cox had steered our boat into the bank. He had lost his concentration by looking back momentarily to see the boat behind us. In that split second we approached a sharp bend in the river and the rest is history. For the first time it dawned on me how important the work of the cox was to the success of our boat.

Often we are guilty of desiring uniformity rather than unity. We think, "If I could only sing like Sue," or "If I could only teach like Bill." It isn't necessary for you to be like anyone else for you to be important to the ministry of the body. It is only important that you fulfill the specific task for which God created and gifted you. It is our diversity that creates unity.

Principle 5:
Gifts Make Us Interdependent

The phrase "individually members of one another" (v. 5) breaks the parallelism with verse 4 and thus stands out in bold relief. The spiritual gifts cause us to be interdependent. A part of our fallen human nature drives us to independence. From the child who pulls away from the mother's grasp to declare, "I can do it myself" to the young adult who defiantly asserts, "I don't need you or anyone else!" we all struggle with the desire for independence. It's true that, in some ways, we must cut the umbilical cord of dependence, but it is equally true that we were created as relational beings and will always stand in need of community.

Today much of the material on developing one's self-image is often self-centered. It caters to this desire for independence and ignores the need for fellowship and family. Discovering and understanding our self-identity will not lead us to arrogant isolation, but to responsible community living. When we discover who we are in Christ, we won't have to be all things to all people. The compulsion to prove ourselves worthy will no longer be an overwhelming quest of life. We won't be tempted to trample on others on our way up the ladder of personal identity and success.

The proper understanding of God's grace and the function of spiritual gifts makes me aware of my unique self-identity and my total dependence. These are not contradictory concepts; they are two sides of the same coin. By virtue of creation and redemption, I am dependent upon God's grace for all that I am or have. By virtue of my giftedness I am dependent upon other members of the body of Christ to complete me and minister to me. I need you and you need me. Your gift ministers to me and your gift completes mine and enables us both to serve in the context of God's family. We do not lose our self-identity by confessing our interdependence. On the contrary, we begin to discover it.

Discovering and understanding our self-identity
will not lead us to arrogant isolation, but to
responsible community living.

We are so interrelated that when one member suffers, we all suffer together. When one rejoices we all rejoice together. None of us can develop a healthy self-image apart from the body. The gifted member severed from the body soon becomes lifeless and useless. We might watch a gifted pianist and comment that he or she has gifted hands. Those hands separated from the whole of the body would serve no purpose. All of us have watched gifted athletes who have lost the perspective of the role of the entire team in their success. They soon become ineffective, isolated, and sullen. We cannot function independently because God created us, uniquely gifted us, and placed us in the body just as He chose. When you discover His divine purpose for your life, then you will know your unique self-image.

Principle 6:
Gifts Serve the Common Good

You are gifted so that you might discover your meaningful existence in God's design. Nothing will give greater purpose and meaning to your life than the recognition of your gifted potential to serve the common good. The spirituals in Corinth arrogantly believed that the gifts proved that they were spiritually elite. They displayed their gifts in such a way that they were tearing down their own body, the church. Gifts have no value unless they edify the body and serve God's divine purpose.

God has sovereignly equipped His body for any task in every new generation. No task is too great for the church who assists its members in discovering and employing their individual gifts. You can be assured that you are a part of God's gifted plan! You are created to be a colaborer with Him! No person is unimportant or insignificant to the mission task! No task that God calls you to do is mundane or insignificant! If it's important to God, it's important!

When you catch the vision of being an integral gifted part of God's eternal purpose, it will truly be life-changing. God will not ask you to do that which He will not enable you to do. Look again in the mirror before you. Do you believe that God would lie to you? Then you must believe God when He tells you that He has created you and placed you in the church just as He chose. *You are a gifted person!*

Nothing will give greater purpose and meaning to your life than the recognition of your gifted potential to serve the common good.

Reflections in the Mirror

1. A personal relationship with God through Christ is the first step in discovering your self-image. Do you know for certain that you have received Jesus Christ as your personal Savior? If not, look at appendix A on page 190 and make that decision right now. If you are a Christian, take a moment to thank God for giving you new life.

2. The gifts function in the context of your physical body which God made alive the moment you were saved. God calls us to present our bodies as living sacrifice so that He can fully empower us and use us in His service. Are you willing to do that? As a sacrifice you offer yourself to the Lord and surrender to Him your time, your service, your all. Pray right now in your own words a prayer of commitment to the Lord.

3. The church has been called the largest volunteer ministry organization in the world. This is not quite true. Our service is not an issue of volunteerism, but of living sacrifice. As Christians we are gifted and called to service. Are you willing to accept God's calling for you and serve at His command?

4. Develop the practice of renewing your mind daily through prayer and regular study of God's Word. The world tells us that our self-image is based in physical attributes, worldly success, or other things. The Bible teaches us that a healthy self-image is found in living in a manner that is pleasing to our Creator. Do you believe God or the world?

5. Two dangers involved in determining and using our gifts are overevaluation leading to arrogance and underevaluation leading to uselessness. Which side of the coin do you find yourself struggling with?

6. God has designed us to be interdependent and not independent. Do you have an independent spirit based on false pride that is hindering you from discovering your true self-image? Have you made a commitment to find your place in the body of Christ? Thank God that He thinks you are valuable enough to have created you with unique purpose for His body.

Do you believe that God would lie to you? Then you must believe God when He tells you that He has created you and placed you in the church just as He chose.

7. Many self-help books point us to positive thinking as the key for self-image. Positive thinking, however, does not provide the empowering necessary to accomplish the task. The Holy Spirit does indwell the Christian to empower him/her for service. Do you remember the seven foundation stones for a positive self-image? List them.

8. List the six principles of giftedness found in Romans 12.

Do you believe these principles are true? You are gifted!

Turning the Kaleidoscope

One of the most innovative and beautiful uses of mirrors occurs in the kaleidoscope. With the use of multiple mirror images the kaleidoscope can make everyday objects beautiful beyond description.

A few years ago I visited a shop in Asheville, North Carolina, that specializes in kaleidoscopes. I couldn't believe the immense variety of kaleidoscopes now available. My primitive notion of a cardboard tube with bits of colored plastic had been surpassed by gleaming silver and bronze cylinders with a dazzling variety of objects which could be refracted into beautiful kaleidoscopic scenes by twisting a tube or spinning a wheel. Some of the models had brightly colored marbles attached to the end of the tube while others had bits of glass, wildflowers, and other assorted bits of nature. When I viewed the object on which the kaleidoscope focused without the benefit of the kaleidoscopic mirror images, they were rather ordinary, but through the mirrored tube they took on a surreal beauty.

I hope that our study of spiritual gifts has been for you as exciting as my visit to the kaleidoscope shop. Viewed alone and unrefracted by the kaleidoscope's mirrors, you may have thought of yourself as rather ordinary and unimpressive. Now as we twist the barrel to one final biblical passage, I trust you will see the incredible beauty of your gifted self-image.

The Ephesian Letter

The Ephesian letter will provide our last major passage. It contains a frequently quoted passage about the working of the gifted body: "He gave some, . . . as pastors and teachers, for the equipping of the saints for the work of service, to the building up of the body of Christ" (4:11). But how does that work? How do gifted members and gifted leaders work together to provide a beautiful kaleidoscopic picture of God's gifted body?

The general tone of this letter and the lack of personal remembrances makes it unlikely that Ephesians was written to a singular congregation, particularly one known to Paul. Notice, for example, that in 3:1-2 Paul introduced himself by including a reference to his ministry to the Gentiles. Such a reference would hardly be necessary in a church where Paul had ministered for at least two years (Acts 19:1-20).

Why was this letter written, and to whom? While Paul was in prison, he came into contact with Epaphras (Col. 4:12), who was a leader in the church at Colossae (1:7-8). Epaphras shared with Paul that heretical teachings were creating difficulties for his church in Colossae and requested his assistance. Therefore, Paul wrote Colossians at the request of Epaphras. In that letter he dealt with the difficulties at Colossae in a straightforward and specific manner.

The news that heretical teachings were affecting this congregation caused Paul to be concerned for the church at Ephesus and other churches throughout proconsular Asia. It is not unlikely that many of the churches in Asia Minor owed their origin to Paul's work in Ephesus. Thus, having written a specific letter to the church at Colossae, Paul seized the opportunity to write a more general and positive letter with the specific intention of stopping the spread of similar heretical teachings throughout Asia Minor.

Paul dispatched Tychicus, a beloved brother and faithful servant with these two letters (4:7), but one complicating factor remained. Paul had another visitor in prison, Onesimus, a runaway slave. Paul had led Onesimus to Christ and now he was a "beloved brother" (v. 9), but Paul felt compelled to return him to his owner, Philemon. Paul desired that Onesimus be freed and treated as a brother, but the fact remained that he was presently a runaway.

Tychicus, accompanied by Onesimus and bearing three letters; Ephesians, Colossians, and Philemon, traveled by sea, landing at Ephesus. Here he delivered the letter we know as Ephesians with the instructions that it should be shared with other churches of proconsular Asia. It would have been natural for a letter from Paul intended to strengthen the churches in Asia Minor to originate from this central seaport location which had been the focal point of Paul's ministry in Asia.

I would further suggest that the original route for the distribution of the letter was the seven churches mentioned in the Book of Revelation: Ephesus, Smyrna, Pergamum, Thyatira, Sardis, Philadelphia, and Laodicea. These churches may have banded together for fellowship and friendship, forming a vital communication link for early believers. Thus after Tychicus delivered the Ephesian letter, he proceeded with the runaway slave directly to Colossae and Philemon by way of the Meander Valley. This route would have been more direct and less populous, providing greater safety for the runaway.

There are several verses in these two letters which make this reconstruction very appealing. According to Colossians 4:15-16, Paul wanted the Colossians to share their letter with the Laodiceans and to read the letter from Laodicea. Laodicea would have been the final stop on the route suggested above. The letter from Laodicea is the letter we know as Ephesians. In the Colossian letter Paul expressed his concern for "all those who have not personally seen my face" (2:1), and he directed the Colossians to share this letter with the Laodiceans (4:16). Could it be that Paul wanted the Colossian letter shared with an even larger audience? The churches which received Ephesians were promised a personal visit by Tychicus (Eph. 6:21-22). Tychicus, after his first mission, could visit each of the seven churches, carrying a copy of the Colossian letter. He could explain the purpose of these unexpected Pauline Epistles and further encourage the churches. It is not by accident that these two letters complement and explain one another.

Identifying the Problem

Since heresy prompted Paul to write Ephesians, it would be helpful to understand what the heresy was. By reading both letters we discover a community which was under pressure to conform to the beliefs and practices of its pagan and Jewish neighbors. Some teachers claimed to possess a deep wisdom and insight into the will of God. They may have based these claims on visionary experiences. They did not give Christ the exalted place accorded Him in Christian teaching (Col. 1:15-20 and 2:8-10). This devaluation of Christ presented a challange to the validity and historical continuity of the church. Was the church nothing more than another religious sect? The uniqueness of the church and the uniqueness of Christ are inextricably bound together.

To combat this heresy Paul assured the readers that Christ was the full expression of God and that the church was built on the foundation of the holy apostles and prophets. That phrase was intended to grant assurance to the struggling communities by underlining the historical continuity of the church and the authority of Paul's message. In Colossians the prominent theme was the authority and dominion of Christ over the universe (Col. 1:13-23). In the Ephesian letter, Paul applied this same theme to affirm these threatened communities by demonstrating the ongoing relationship of Christ, who is Lord over all things, to the church (1:20-23). The message of the Ephesian letter not only challenges us to refuse to play church, but it reminds us of the significance of our spiritual gifts in the divine strategy of world redemption.

The Context of Ephesians 4

"Therefore" in 4:1 indicates a link between the discussion which follows and the material which preceded. Paul's first exhortation in this final gift passage was to live in a manner worthy of our calling. This exhortation was based on truths already explained: they had been chosen (1:4), called (v. 18), and made alive by God's grace (2:5). The Ephesians must never forget that they were once "sons of disobedience" (v. 2), but God who is "rich in mercy" (v. 4) had enabled them to enter into relationship with Himself (vv. 5-10) and thus they were now members of God's household. This household was built upon the foundation of the apostles and prophets, with Christ Himself as the cornerstone.

In chapter 3 Paul, with great wonder and humility, had reminded them of his own calling to preach the gospel. It was this radical understanding of grace which had enabled a former persecutor, a man who considered himself to be least of all saints (v. 8), to boldly preach the unfathomable riches of Christ. The grace encounter is always the beginning of developing a healthy self-image that will enable us to participate in God's plan of world redemption.

God had enabled Paul to preach so that He might now make known His manifold wisdom through the church. This mystery, now revealed, was planned in the heart of God before the foundation of the world and carried out in Christ Jesus. And it is by virtue of our relationship with Christ that "we have boldness and confident access through faith in Him" (v. 12). Does the idea of "boldness" and "confident access" sound a little intimidating to you? It shouldn't! This is what God did for you in Christ Jesus. If you can boldly look God in the face, why should you quake before mere humans?

Paul burst into impassioned prayer that the Ephesians would come to possess the full empowering of God. He prayed that they would be strengthened with power in the inner man—a strength that was according to the riches of His glory. He asked that they would be able to comprehend the love of Christ which surpasses knowing. It is our relationship with "all the saints" (v. 18) that enables us to know the unknowable love of Christ. Finally, Paul prayed that the reader would be filled up to the fullness of God. As we turn the kaleidoscope once again we can't help but be impressed with the unfathomable riches available to us. This is the stuff that builds lasting self-esteem.

The incredible truth of who we are in Christ forms the basis for the requirements of chapters 4—6. It is the foundation for unity, mutual service, the demand for moral integrity, and unity in the home. Thus we notice once again that the actual discussion of gifts for ministry (4:7-16) is both preceded and followed by ethical instruction and bound to the total life of the church. We will discover both our gifts and our own unique identity in the context of the loving family of Christ. Let's look at the last few truths that will provide the necessary understanding for discovering and using our gifts.

The grace encounter is always the beginning of developing a healthy self-image that will enable us to participate in God's plan of world redemption.

My Walk in Community

Throughout our study we have discovered the importance of community for our personal development, and this passage is no different. The description of the worthy walk begins in 4:2 with the phrase; "showing forbearance to one another in love." Love alone will enable us to overcome the dangers inherent in human relationships. We must learn to live together harmoniously as family if we are going to develop a good self-image.

This verse is not about being virtuous, but about living in harmony with God's call. We could compare this verse to the fruit of the Spirit because these attributes are produced by the Spirit of God in the life of the person who has been saved by grace and has become the workmanship of God. Don't fall into the trap of trying to produce these virtues by human striving. When we try to be patient or kind on our own, we simply become more discouraged in our inability to change. These virtues are the divine work of the Spirit and thus come through surrender.

Humility and gentleness are linked together in the Greek construction. Humility is a distinctly biblical virtue. It was actually considered a vice in the Greek world. Humility is not a pious, personal put-down. It does not require us to declare: "Oh, I'm just a nobody. I'm not important to the church." Often such remarks are little more than inverted conceit. They beg for human affirmation and neglect the voice of God who calls us His beloved. Humility is the opposite of complacency, conceit, and self-exaltation. Humility is actually the *proper evaluation* of myself based on the understanding that I am totally dependent upon the grace of God. Proper evaluation of self rules out both arrogance and self-pity and enables us to be gentle in relationship with others.

We must learn to live together harmoniously as family if we are going to develop a good self-image.

Humility, gentleness, and patience are the divine attributes, the practical expressions of love, which enable believers to forbear with one another in love and thus to preserve the unity of the Spirit (v. 3). It is love in all its practical expressions which must govern the Christian life and specifically personal relationships in the body of Christ. This theme is amplified in verses 17-32, where we are reminded that we must be renewed in the spirit of the mind, put on the new self, and behave accordingly because we are members of one another.

Don't forget that this theme of community has been repeated in every gift passage. In 1 Thessalonians, Paul admonished the brethren to esteem their leaders in love, to live in peace, to help the weak, to be patient with all, and to show forbearance when wronged. Faced with the exaggerated claims of the spirituals, Paul placed the description of the authentic spiritual person at the heart of the discussion of gifts in 1 Corinthians 13. He then proceeded in chapter 14 to demonstrate the practical effects of the outworking of love in the life of the gifted community. In Romans, Paul placed the discussion of gifts in the context of ethical behavior and underlined the necessity for proper evaluation of ourselves. We cannot ignore this repeated lesson. Gifts have meaning only in the context of community. To be used in an authentic manner they must express God's grace through the edification of the brethren.

If we are going to work together as a gifted family, we must have unity. Why did Paul, in one breath say that Christians are given unity and in the very next breath exhort the readers to preserve the unity of the Spirit? Paul boldly affirmed the unity of all believers by denoting seven great unifying truths Christians hold in common. Yet he challenged the gifted members to labor together, "until we all attain to the unity of the faith" (v. 13). Unity is at once a given, but must be maintained by all the gifted members working together in harmony.

Humility is actually the **proper evaluation** *of myself based on the understanding that I am totally dependent upon the grace of God.*

The sevenfold expression of unity is one of the most eloquent compositions in all of Scripture. The first triad—one body, one Spirit, one hope of your calling—recalls several concepts discussed in the early chapters of this letter (v. 4). "One body" refers to the church as the body of Christ and "one Spirit" refers to the Holy Spirit who indwells the members of the church and gives it unity. The church is a spiritual organism, made up of persons who have in common the shared experience of the Spirit. Thus it derives its life, unity, and ministries from the Spirit, who is the gift of the ascended Lord. "One hope of your calling" means the hope which is received by virtue of one's response to the call to salvation. By virtue of our relationship to Christ we have been given purpose for living (cf. 1:18).

The second triad—one Lord, one faith, and one baptism— reminds the readers of the moment when they confessed Jesus as Lord as they descended into the water of baptism. This common relationship to Christ shared through baptism had broken down all barriers that could be divisive. This truth was clearly underlined by Paul in the Corinthian gift passage: "For by one Spirit we were all baptized into one body" (1 Cor. 12:13). Paul concluded this series of seven truths with a reference to God, whose oneness is the basis for the unity of His people.

While Paul stressed that unity is a gift of God mediated by the Holy Spirit, he nevertheless impressed on his readers that it was also a goal toward which the church must strive. The phrase, "being diligent to preserve the unity of the Spirit," reminded the readers that although they could not create unity, they must make every effort to preserve it. Unity must be pursued through the edifying use of the gifts. The final phrase of verse 3, "in the bond of peace" indicated that peace would be the end result of living in love.

It is a sad commentary that our distorted understanding of gifts has often led to disunity in the body of Christ rather than preserving the unity of the Spirit. When gifts are properly understood as manifestations of grace, sought with edification of the body in mind, and used for the good of the whole, the result will be humility, unity, edification, and peace. When gifts are properly appreciated and used, personal growth and church growth will follow.

The Gifts of the Exalted Lord

The giving of the gifts in this letter was related to the exalted Lord. Once again we are reminded that all believers are gifted: "But to each one of us grace was given according to the measure of Christ's gift" (v. 7). Paul did not use the word *charismata,* but he used the root *charis* along with another Greek word that means gift.

Paul didn't have the same hang-ups with terminology that we do today. We hear someone use the phrases "charismatic church" or "Spirit-filled Christian," and we immediately draw lines that divide. How contrary this is to the teaching of the New Testament. Every believer and every church is by spiritual birth charismatic in the true biblical sense. This does not necessitate that they speak in tongues or practice the gift of healing. It means that they have experienced the grace of the Lord Jesus Christ in salvation, and they possess the individualized grace of God empowering them for ministry in the world. Without this gracious empowering no ministry can be accomplished in any church. This should warn believers of all denominations to avoid labels and their judgmental implications.

The emphasis on the exalted Christ as the giver of gifts is both unique and central to this passage. In Corinthians, where there was an exaggerated spirituality, Paul paid particular attention to the ministry of the Holy Spirit in the gifting of each and every believer. He noted the one Spirit's ministry in creating unity in the body, fostered by the diversity of gifts which He distributed to each one individually as He wills. In Romans, where Paul wrote with no particular problem in mind, he made no explicit mention of the Spirit's role in dispersing the gifts. The stress was on God as the Author of the gifts.

It is a sad commentary that our distorted understanding of gifts has often led to disunity in the body of Christ rather than preserving the unity of the Spirit.

Christ's authority as the giver of the gifts was supported by a paraphrased reference to Psalm 68:18. The paraphrase Paul used contained the phrase "He gave gifts to men" rather than "Thou hast received gifts among men." This change was important since it established the point that Christ was the one who gave gifts to persons. The emphasis on the exaltation of Christ, His dominion over all powers, and His filling of all things is consistently emphasized in Colossians and Ephesians. Now by applying this psalm to Christ, Paul underlined the total sufficiency of the exalted Lord who Himself made the church sufficient for any task. This struck a telling blow against the heresy that would devalue Christ and thus His church.

Christ, who previously descended, has triumphed over all powers, including death, and has been highly exalted in virtue of which He fills all things. The phrase, "He led captive a host of captives" (v. 8) is a reference to Christ's dominion over all spirits and powers which previously ruled over humanity (cf. 1:21). It is the exalted, triumphant Christ Himself who equips the church with gifted persons for victorious world-changing ministry. This single truth, when fully accepted, should be sufficient to shake us from the lethargy of playing church. It should affirm us in our God-given self-image.

Paul expressed a similar idea in Colossians 2:14-15. I love the *New English Bible's* translation of this verse. "On that cross he discarded the cosmic powers and authorities like a garment; he made a public spectacle of them and led them as captives in his triumphal procession." The triumph of Christ was in Colossians related to the freedom of the believer (vv. 16-18) and to Christ's ability as the head of the body to supply everything necessary for the growth of the church (v. 19). The empowering of the church was a more prominent theme in Ephesians and what Paul mentioned in Colossians 2:19, he fully explained in Ephesians 4:7-16.

These believers were not members of an insignificant religious sect, but a part of the triumphant church which was fully equipped by the Lord of the universe. Anyone tempted to believe that there were other avenues to divine fullness should realize that the fullness of the Godhead dwells in Christ and that He alone fills heaven and earth. Paul's insistence that Christ is the giver of the gifts was related to this unique historical situation, but this truth applies today. There is no greater source for developing a positive self-image than the recognition that you are a gifted member of the triumphant body of Christ. As a gifted body member, you are Christ's gift to the church. Some mirror!

Gifted Leaders to Equip Gifted Saints

As we turn our kaleidoscope we see a unique facet fall into view as Paul described the relationship between gifted leaders and gifted members. All members are still viewed as being uniquely gifted (4:7), and all must work together for the proper growth of the body. The leaders, however, are body members who have gifts and responsibilities for enabling other gifted members to do the work of service.

Some Christians seem to think that pastors are the only persons in the church able to do ministry. If someone is sick, their first thought is to send the pastor. If they have an unsaved friend—the pastor should go. Early in my ministry I was teaching a class on personal evangelism in a small country church where I served. I had just completed this particular course in another church where I had been a member. I knew it would work, and I knew it was just the ticket to help us reach our community. Attendance was excellent for the first few weeks and then it declined suddenly and rapidly. I was frustrated and fell into the trap of preaching to the persons present about the lack of commitment of those who were missing.

A deacon raised his hand and asked, "Preacher why are you teaching us about witnessing? We pay you to do that."

I was stunned! Suddenly, I felt like a hired gun. "Preacher, you're the professional. We hired you to go get the bad guys." Few people will be as honest as that deacon was that night. Yet the feeling that the pastor is the only person in the church qualified to minister has paralyzed the church, burned the pastor out, and kept many gifted laypeople from experiencing the true joy of using their gifts in meaningful ministry. I'm not suggesting that the pastor shouldn't visit the hospitals or lost people. He should. I am merely echoing the scriptural principle that all the members of the body are gifted to minister.

The ministry of the New Testament church is a shared ministry in which the pastor is one gifted member who helps other gifted members to recognize, develop, and use their God-given talents for ministry. It does not create a conflict to affirm that individuals are gifted and yet insist that they must be equipped for the work of service. The verb that Paul used contained both the idea of "preparing" and "making complete." Thus to say that Christians are gifted does not suggest that they do not need further teaching and training in order to fully utilize their gifts. We recognize this principle when we encourage a person who feels called to full-time ministry to go to seminary to complete his or her training. Now we must apply this principle to the entire church family. When we discover gifted teachers, we shouldn't arm them with a quarterly and thrust them headlong into a room of fifth graders. They need and deserve to be further equipped. Spiritual gifts are given by the Spirit but can be developed by use and training.

There is no greater source for developing a positive self-image than the recognition that you are a gifted member of the triumphant body of Christ.

The gift list in Ephesians 4 is unique, containing a twofold emphasis—gifts are given to persons (vv. 7-8) and, in turn, these gifted persons are given to the church (v. 11). This is not unlike the emphasis of 1 Corinthians 12:28; "And God has appointed in the church first apostles, second prophets, third teachers." Even more unique is the fact that all the gifts mentioned here are specifically related to leadership functions. Why are only leadership gifts mentioned? The answer is to be found in the specific historical context.

Let's review for a moment what we learned from the earlier gift lists. In the first gift list in 1 Corinthians 12:8-10, Paul included only the "extraordinary" or "ecstatic" gifts which were eagerly sought by the spirituals. Paul's second list in that chapter (v. 28) expanded the Corinthians' understanding of gifts by placing apostles, prophets, and teachers first and adding two rather mundane service gifts, helps and administrations. In Romans 12:6 Paul did not mention the ecstatic gifts, but placed emphasis on service and leadership gifts. Yet none of these lists are the same.

The feeling that the pastor is the only person in the church qualified to minister has paralyzed the church, burned the pastor out, and kept many gifted laypeople from experiencing the true joy of using their gifts in meaningful ministry.

The emphasis on leadership, teaching, and service gifts is again clear in Ephesians 4. The actual gift list was restricted to leadership/ teaching functions because of the particular historical situation. Paul placed apostles, prophets, and other teachers at the center of this passage to counteract the heretical teachings present in proconsular Asia. It is noteworthy that the proper functioning of the gifts was related to doctrinal stability in verse 14. Paul never intended any gift list to be comprehensive, and he quite freely tailored each list to fit the need of the historical situation.

The listing of evangelist and pastor/teacher are new to Paul's lists. We have noticed that "new" gifts have been found in every list. I think that if Paul were to have written about gifts several more times, he would have added other gifts as the situation dictated. Those who attempt to number the spiritual gifts and then group all the various ministries around certain divisions of gifts misunderstand the dynamic nature of Paul's teaching. God uniquely gifts His church for each new task and ministry as the need arises.

Certainly we can affirm that many of the New Testament gifts remain operative as the mission of the church dictates their use. Gifts such as teaching, administration, and showing mercy, to name but a few, will always be needed by the ministering church. Yet with the advent of technological advances, many churches require persons with technical skills and gifts in electronics or sound engineering to help facilitate their ministries. We should not hesitate to think of these God-given abilities for service as spiritual gifts when they are rightly understood as a gracious gifts of God and surrendered to His service for the edification of the body.

In some churches I sense a "we" versus "them" spirit concerning the staff and the people. Some pastors almost unconsciously talk of their people as "those folks." On the other hand, I hear church members refer to the pastor or staff member as a virtual outsider. "We've got to be careful! The staff is always trying to get us to spend our money." The pastor and staff are viewed as an outside influence trying to change the church. We'll never become what God intends us to be until we drop these labels and artificial barriers. We are one body with interrelated gifts and responsibilities. We are inextricably bound together by our gifts and our mutual needs.

The Results of Gifted Ministry

The phrase "to the building up of the body of Christ" (4:12) expressed a goal which was viewed in both a short-range and long-range context. In verse 13 the goal of edification through the proper use of gifts was developed in two directions, both of which were consistent with Paul's concern in the entire letter. Paul desired for them (1) unity of the faith and (2) a full measure of spiritual maturity. These two phrases further define the building up of the body. In verse 14 the proper use of gifts was applied specifically to the immediate danger of false doctrine which threatened these communities. Edifying use of gifts which resulted in unity and maturity would enable them to stand against the pressures of false doctrine.

The phrases "unity of the faith" and "knowledge of the Son of God" are closely tied together. The themes of unity and knowledge received special attention in both Colossians and Ephesians because of the unsettling heretical teachings in proconsular Asia. The emphasis on knowledge and the mention of false teaching indicate that "faith" here must be taken in an objective sense. Personal belief in Christ committed people to the objective truths of sound doctrine (Eph. 4:20-21). Knowledge of this body of truth which they had been taught would give these early Christians stability against false teaching. The teaching of sound doctrine is still the church's mainline defense against heretical teaching and is the real glue that provides for unity.

This letter abounds with references to Paul's desire that his readers grow in the "knowledge of the Son of God." In Ephesians 1:15-23 Paul prayed that they would receive "a spirit of wisdom and of revelation in the knowledge of Him" (v. 17). The "knowledge of Him" was further defined as an understanding of the hope to which they had been called, the riches of His glorious inheritance in the saints, and the immeasurable greatness of His power which is available to the believer. The reference to "the knowledge of the Son of God" in 4:13 contained both the idea of personal relationship with Christ and a full understanding of the riches available to the believer in Christ. Paul wanted them to see how utterly futile it was to search for any spiritual blessing outside of Christ. Why would anyone consider doing so when Christ is the fullness of Him who fills all in all?

It is easier to point out the mistakes of earlier generations than it is to learn from them. Why are so many people looking for spiritual wholeness in cults or psychic phenomena? Why is the New Age movement growing so quickly? Could it be that the church has shown little evidence of the fullness of Christ? Could it be that we have not been taught to appropriate the fullness of Christ?

We must also be wary of the subtle suggestion that some experience must be added to the Christian life in order to receive the fullness of power and blessing. We frequently hear the teaching that we must receive a second act of grace or the baptism of the Spirit subsequent to salvation to know the fullness of God. Paul's emphasis in all of his letters was that the fullness of God was made available in Christ alone. The suggestion that salvation requires any other act to make it complete is a dangerous and nonbiblical emphasis. You may need to come to a more mature knowledge of the Son of God and thus fully open yourself to the fullness already made available in Christ, but God does not withhold any of His fullness. We must all continually and habitually seek the full flow of God's power through us.

The phrase "unity of the faith, and of the knowledge of the Son of God" stresses both the unity of Christian belief, in contrast to the diverse winds of doctrine, and the full sufficiency of Christ in the face of every claim to provide wisdom or spiritual power through another source. Paul made this bold assertion to combat the childish behavior of those who were being blown off course by every wind of doctrine. If they simply sought the fullness of Christ, they would discover the abundance for every good work. They needed only to grow in knowledge, not seek another spiritual experience. Yet the tendency remains. It is easier and more emotionally gratifying to seek a mystical spiritual experience than to accept the discipline necessary to grow in the knowledge of God. Discovering your true identity through your giftedness does not require any emotional experience, but it does require spiritual discipline.

The ultimate and long-term goal of the full utilization of gifts was growth to maturity which is measured by the fullness of Christ. To understand this phrase we must trace it through this letter. In Ephesians 1:20-23 Paul declared that Christ was the fullness of God, "who fills all in all" (v. 23). He noted that God had placed everything in subjection under Christ for the advantage of the church. Paul prayed that the readers would personally experience this fullness of God in terms of inner strengthening, the indwelling presence of Christ, and an overflowing abundance of love (3:14-21). When this abundance is seen in us, it will glorify Christ in the church. Here in Ephesians 4 Paul clarified the way in which this fullness of God was actually experienced in the church. Christ has ascended and descended that He Himself might personally fill all things. He does so through the distribution of gifted persons to the church. The "fullness of Christ" therefore refers to the completeness which is already made available to the bride of Christ, but which must be attained by the full utilization of the gifts. Thus it is at once a "gift" and a "goal," a "blessing" and a "calling."

Why are so many people looking for spiritual wholeness in cults or psychic phenomena? Why is the New Age movement growing so quickly? Could it be that the church has shown little evidence of the fullness of Christ?

This process of growth to maturity is accomplished through the full utilization of the gifts, as each member works according to his or her own measure. It is through the service of the gifted members that the divine energy flows in full power. Paul called Christians of every generation, who might be tempted to seek spiritual fullness elsewhere, to take advantage of the full resources of God already available to them in Christ. As we can readily see much is at stake in the proper understanding of our giftedness.

In verse 14 the goals of total church growth are brought into focus by a sharp contrast with the current historical situation. To be blown about by every wind of doctrine was childish when one understood that the church has the sufficiency of the fullness of Christ. The reference to "every wind of doctrine" (v. 14) spoke of both the pluralistic religious atmosphere in proconsular Asia and also the transitory value of these false teachings when compared to the truth revealed in Christ. These winds will blow themselves out! Those who were seeking after deeper spiritual experiences outside of Christ were compared to small rudderless boats, tossed about freely by the action of the winds and the waves.

I can still remember the first little boats I made as a child. They were simple and rudderless. I would throw them in the creek and run along the bank watching their progress. Actually I spent most of my time wading the creek attempting to free them from the debris that so easily entangled them. Christians without a sound theological foundation are like little rudderless boats. They are easily deceived and are often tossed about or caught up in the debris of false teaching.

How do we guard ourselves and our church from false doctrine? How do we experience the full empowering of Christ? First we must speak the truth in love (v. 15). What a contrast with the scheming false teachers. The spoken truth was necessary to curb the dangerous winds of doctrine swirling through Asia. But speaking truth must occur in the context of love. Notice the repetition of "in love" in verses 15 and 16. "In love" describes the sphere of Christian life and the manner in which all Christian ministry is to take place. The gifted body must grow toward unity and maturity, but it does so in the context of love.

The ultimate goal of growth is summarized in verse 16. Here we look into the inner workings of the community which is in the process of growth. Paul brought together four prominent themes of the passage and related each of them to the present work of the church and the individual believer in the pilgrimage to live up to our high calling.

1. *The church is empowered to grow because Christ, the Lord of the universe, fills it.*—The focus on Christ as the head was intended to direct the reader's attention to the practical ramifications of being part of the body of Christ, who is Lord of the universe. The energy for growth comes from Christ Himself. This truth should forever put to an end the popular refrains, "we can't" or "I can't." The source of your empowering assures you that you can.

2. *Every body member is fully involved in the growth process.*—

The conduit for divine energy is each joint of the body. The joint in the human body serves to magnify and direct the energy supplied by the muscle. The muscle power in the spiritual life is supplied by the Holy Spirit, but the gifted member is the joint by which the energy of the Holy Spirit is magnified and applied to specific earthly needs. The picture is actually that of a lever and fulcrum.

I can remember my dad teaching me how to use a lever and fulcrum. I had been struggling most of the day to remove a stump from the garden. It had been cut free, but I just couldn't seem to remove it by direct force. After watching me struggle for awhile, he showed me how to focus and magnify my energy through the use of a lever and fulcrum. It seemed almost magical to an eight-year-old that such a simple tool could have such a profound impact. You are that channel through which God desires to focus His divine power and apply it in the world today. It is essential that you discover and use your gifts, for God wants to use you as a channel of strength.

Christians without a sound theological foundation
are like little rudderless boats.

3. *Unity is necessary for diversely gifted members to work in harmony.*—The emphasis on *every, each,* and *proper working* stresses the demand for unity and mutual support in the utilization of spiritual gifts. Remember that gifts make us dependent on one another. One body member working alone can accomplish little and will soon become impoverished due to the lack of edification from other body members. You can only discover your true self-image in the context of the family of God.

4. *The full utilization of our gifts must take place in the context of love.*—The fully gifted community is not only distinguished by its full possession of gifts through which divine energy flows, but it is also marked by its divine nature. This should remind us that the fullest expression of any gift without love has no spiritual value (1 Cor. 13). For example, we might find a person who is a gifted teacher, but who does not teach in a spirit of love. No edification would occur in this loveless application of the gift of teaching and, therefore, there would be no growth of the body.

Reflections in the Mirror

1. Were you aware of the historical continuity of the church? Did you know that the church was so vital in God's strategy for world redemption? How does it make you feel to be gifted and called to minister through the church? _____

2. You are a vital part of God's family. You belong! Living in the family requires a spirit of love with gentleness and patience. These cannot be conjured up through human effort, but they are made possible by the indwelling presence of the Holy Spirit. What relational attitude do you most need for the Holy Spirit to develop in your life?

_____

3. How does it make you feel about inherent worth to know that you are a gift of the risen and exalted Lord to the church? _____

_____

4. You are as much called to ministry as is your pastor or other staff member. Yet they have a unique role to help you to discover, develop, and use your gifts. Have you asked these persons for assistance in your gift discovery?

5. List the results of every-member ministry?

_____

Where can you make the greatest contribution in the life of your church? _____

6. Do you remember the seven building blocks for self-worth? Before we move to the chapter on gift discovery, let's take the self-image assessment once again. Compare the results with the survey you completed earlier.

The fullest expression of any gift without love has no spiritual value.

Self-image Scale

Directions:
Circle the number that most represents
your present feelings about yourself
1 = Never   5 = Always

1. I feel good about myself.   1 2 3 4 5

2. I feel secure.   1 2 3 4 5

3. I feel I know myself well.   1 2 3 4 5

4. I know what I want out of life.   1 2 3 4 5

5. I am accepted by others.   1 2 3 4 5

6. I feel able to handle my situation.   1 2 3 4 5

7. I am confident in my ability to perform.   1 2 3 4 5

8. I base my feelings about myself on my   1 2 3 4 5
   worth, not my performance.

9. I have a sense of peace even in the midst of   1 2 3 4 5
   adversity.

10. I like who I am.   1 2 3 4 5

11. My commitments are based on my   1 2 3 4 5
    priorities.

12. I feel that I am welcome in my social   1 2 3 4 5
    groups.

13. I feel like I have control of my destiny.   1 2 3 4 5

14. I feel that I can accomplish anything I set   1 2 3 4 5
    my mind to do.

15. I feel good about myself even when I have   1 2 3 4 5
    made mistakes in my life.

16. I know that no matter what happens I will   1 2 3 4 5
    be OK.

17. I understand who I am.   1 2 3 4 5

18. I have specific goals for my life and   1 2 3 4 5
    evaluate them on an ongoing basis.

19. I feel that I am accepted for who I am, not   1 2 3 4 5
    what I do.

20. I have the ability to accomplish great   1 2 3 4 5
    things.

21. I am knowledgeable and competent in my   1 2 3 4 5
    work.

Scoring

Place the appropriate value for each answer in the appropriate box below. When you have completed each box, total across. After completing each total box add down to get your grand total score.

  Total

Inherent Worth	1 ___	8 ___	15 ___	___	*If you scored:*
Sense of Security	2 ___	9 ___	16 ___	___	15-13 = Excellent
Self-Concept	3 ___	10 ___	17 ___	___	12-10 = Good
Sense of Purpose	4 ___	11 ___	18 ___	___	9- 7 = Fair
Sense of Belonging	5 ___	12 ___	19 ___	___	6- = Poor
Sense of Empower- ment	6 ___	13 ___	20 ___	___	
Feeling of Personal Competence	7 ___	14 ___	21 ___	___	

                                                        Grand Total _____

                    Self-image

Total Self-image Score

If your Grand Total score was
>   85-105   —Your self-image is *excellent*
>   57- 84   —Your self-image is *good*
>   43- 56   —Your self-image is *average*
>   22- 42   —Your self-image is *fair*
>   21-Below—Your self-image is *poor*

Looking at Yourself in God's Mirror

My wife, Paula, is a cytotechnologist. She spends hours with her eye glued to a microscope looking at human body cells. Her microscope is quite a sophisticated and powerful instrument unlike the toy microscopes that came with the Junior Scientist Kits. I can still remember my first microscope. Spurred on by Mister Wizard, I put everything under the lens of my toy microscope. Feathers, butterfly wings, and even an ordinary housefly took on extraordinary proportions and unexpected beauty when viewed under the microscope. That mirrored instrument opened up a whole new world for me.

We have spent several chapters together looking at the perfect mirror of God's Word. It is one thing to read and study about spiritual gifts, but quite another to actually discover and employ them in the local church. This chapter calls us to put our lives under the microscope to find that even the ordinary in our lives, when viewed under God's microscope, becomes quite extraordinary.

Many believers do not use their gifts because they have not been taught how to discover them. Others have fears that have kept them from seeking and using their gifts. It is my hope that this chapter will assist in dispelling any remaining fears that you may have and give you practical steps for discovering your image in Christ through your God-given gifts. I trust that this chapter will prove to be a wonderful pilgrimage for you.

Why Are Gifts So Important?

You may still have some questions as to the relative importance of spiritual gifts. "Are they that important? Can I be fulfilled and productive as a Christian and not know my spiritual gift? If gifts are vital to the life of the church, why wasn't I taught about them earlier? I've gotten along sufficiently well without them for all these years, why should I bother with spiritual gifts now?'' These are all relevant and practical questions. Some have been answered in our study, but others need to be confronted fairly and honestly now.

It is one thing to read and study about spiritual gifts, but quite another to actually discover and employ them in the local church.

1. *Gifts are important because they are a gracious expression of the Father's love for His children.*—God would not give His children anything which was not essential to their spiritual development. Jesus encouraged His disciples to pray boldly with this strong word of assurance: "Or what man is there among you, when his son shall ask him for a loaf, will give him a stone? Of if he shall ask for a fish, he will not give him a snake, will he? If you then, being evil, know how to give good gifts to your children, how much more shall your Father who is in heaven give what is good to those who ask Him!" (Matt. 7:9-11). In Luke's Gospel we discover the same encouragement to pray, but with this conclusion: "If you then, being evil, know how to give good gifts to your children, how much more shall your heavenly Father give the Holy Spirit to those who ask Him?" (11:13) The Christian has no cause to fear the work of the Holy Spirit. God's desire in giving gifts is to enrich your life and to enable you to make a significant contribution to His work. It is important for you to know about spiritual gifts because they are your spiritual heritage. God desires your abundance in the giving of gifts. We should therefore desire to know our gifts because they are the personalized expression of God's grace to us as His children.

2. *Gifts are important because they enable every Christian to participate in fulfilling the Great Commission.*—The Great Commission is succinctly stated in Matthew 28:19-20: "Go therefore and make disciples of all the nations, baptizing them in the name of the Father and the Son and the Holy Spirit, teaching them to observe all that I commanded you; and lo, I am with you always, even to the end of the age." This command is the marching orders of the church and is equally binding on every individual member of each church. Yet many Christians feel that they can do little, other than give their

mission offering, to assist their own church in the fulfilling of the Great Commission. Spiritual gifts are the individualized expression of God's grace for the empowering of every believer to actively and significantly participate in the fulfillment of the Great Commission. If you will notice, the Commission requires evangelistic outreach, careful follow-up, and lifelong teaching and encouragement. Church was never intended to be a spectator sport. You can and must play a significant role in the ministry of your church.

Peter Wagner has creatively related the spiritual gifts to church growth. He correctly notes that the gifts are never an end in themselves, but they are a means toward an end, and that end is the implementation of the Great Commission. Wagner believes that the ignorance concerning spiritual gifts may be a chief cause of retarded church growth today.[1] You have been gifted because God desires to use you as He builds His church.

We often hear the statistic that only about 20 percent of the active members of the local church are involved in the actual ministries of that church. If that is true, and I suspect it is, we should not be surprised to hear that the average local church has either plateaued or is now actually declining in the midst of worldwide spiritual hunger and opportunity. Let's trace the implications of this with a simple example. Most churches expect that about one half of their enrollment will be "active," meaning that they attend somewhat regularly. Of that active group, they further expect that only 50 percent of those will be present on a given Sunday. Out of this group only 20 percent will actually contribute meaningfully to the mission of the church.

What if you were a football coach who had one hundred players on the beginning roster. When it came down to receiving a uniform, only half (fifty) showed up to pick up their uniform. On the night of the first game, only half of those who got their uniforms showed up for that particular game (twenty-five). During the coin toss you discovered that only 20 percent of those who showed up had any intention of playing. The rest declared their intention to be observers. How many games do you think you would win with only five players? You might be inclined to argue that the final twenty-five who showed up for the game would do much better than the 20 percent participation rate. Let's be gracious and double that figure and you will still have only ten players. Let's bring this illustration back to the church. Most church buildings are not designed to accommodate the entire membership if they all attended on the same Sunday.

I do not believe that the average church member is lazy or apathetic about spiritual matters or about fulfilling the Great Commission. In the conferences that I conduct, I have found most Christians eager to learn how they can help their church to grow. I think that our failure to assist believers in discovering and using their gifts accounts for much of the lack of involvement in most churches. Many members do not understand their unique giftedness nor their importance to the proper functioning of their church.

Spiritual gifts are the individualized expression of God's grace for the empowering of every believer to actively and significantly participate in the fulfillment of the Great Commission.

3. *Spiritual gifts lead to purposeful membership in the body of Christ.*—One of my friends in the fourth grade had an extra finger on one hand. When I first saw it, I was stunned. I reacted like the typical fourth grader, calling attention to this extra appendage in a loud voice. I didn't mean any harm; I actually thought it was pretty neat. Who couldn't use an extra finger? My friend was embarrassed by the attention his extra appendage drew from the gawking crowd of fourth graders. I later discovered that his extra finger was actually useless, continually got in his way, and made him feel like a freak. Do you ever feel like an extra and unnecessary appendage? I continually hear well-meaning believers bemoan the fact that they can't do anything. "Pastor, I'll attend and I'll pray, but I'm not able to do anything in the church."

What a tragedy that so many people feel a lack of ability concerning their involvement in the local church! It certainly must have a negative impact on their spiritual self-esteem. Beyond that, it hampers the work of the church. Most of the inactive people on our rolls become dropout statistics because they never became involved in the ministry of the church. They don't feel that they belong! They don't understand that they are a vital and gifted member who has been placed in the body by the sovereign activity of God. "But now God has placed the members, each one of them, in the body, just as He desired" (1 Cor. 12:18). Does "each one" include you? It certainly does! You are not a member of your church by accident. God put you there for a purpose. He gifted you for meaningful service in the life of His body.

4. *Spiritual gifts are important because they enrich your personal life.*—You are a person of value. God has Himself chosen you for service in His body. Let that sink in! How does that make you feel about yourself? About God? About service in your church?

In the little booklet *How to Be Filled with the Spirit,* Dr. Bill Bright relates the story of the vast oil field known as Yates Pool.

During the depression this field was a sheep ranch owned by a man named Yates. Mr. Yates wasn't able to make enough on his ranching operation to pay the principal and interest on the mortgage, so he was in danger of losing his ranch. With little money for clothes or food, his family (like many others) had to live on government subsidy.

Day after day, as he grazed his sheep over those rolling west Texas hills, he was no doubt greatly troubled about how he would pay his bills. Then a seismographic crew from an oil company told him that there might be oil on his land. They asked permission to drill a wildcat well and he signed a lease contract.

At 1,115 feet they struck a huge oil reserve. The first well came in at 80,000 barrels a day. Many subsequent wells were more than twice as large. In fact, 30 years after the discovery, a government test of one of the wells showed that it still had the potential flow of 125,000 barrels of oil a day. And Mr. Yates owned it all! The day he purchased the land he had received the oil and mineral rights. Yet, he'd been living on relief. A multimillionaire living in poverty! The problem? He didn't know the oil was there, even though he owned it.[2]

Church was never intended to be a spectator sport.

That story is one of those good news–bad news accounts. The good news was that Mr. Yates owned incredible financial resources. The bad news was that he spent many unnecessary years in virtual poverty because he didn't know the oil was there. Many Christians waste years of opportunity for fruitful service because they don't know about the wonderful resources that have been provided for them by God through the Holy Spirit. This does not just include inactive church members, but it may also include many members who are serving the Lord out of duty, but with an inadequate understand-

ing of spiritual gifts. When you serve outside the area of your giftedness, it often leads to fatigue and depression.

5. *Spiritual gifts provide for unity in the church.*—The gifts are
given by God for the common good of the body. The gifts thus enable
one member to encourage and edify another. This, in turn, enables
the church to grow in maturity and unity. Gifts, by their very nature,
make us interdependent and, thus, create the necessity and possibil-
ity for unity. Fellowship and unity become the very ground for the
effective operation of the gifts and at the same moment, the full operation of the gifts provides for the unity of the church.

*You are not a member of your church by accident.
God put you there for a purpose.*

Why Do So Few Christians Understand?

If spiritual gifts are critical to the life of the church, why do so few
Christians seem to understand gifts? Why do so few people know
how to identify their gifts? Those are certainly relevant questions and
deserve to be answered. I think there are three basic reasons for the
lack of understanding—1) Failure to Study, 2) Fear of the Unknown,
and 3) Fog of Confusion.

Failure to Study

Paul instructed Timothy: "Be diligent to present yourself ap-
proved to God as a workman who does not need to be ashamed,
handling accurately the word of truth" (2 Tim. 2:15). That admonition could well be applied to the matter of spiritual gifts. When Paul
wrote the Corinthians concerning spiritual gifts, he began: "Now
concerning spiritual gifts, brethren, I do not want you to be un-
aware" (1 Cor. 12:1). The Corinthians, in their spiritual arrogance,
thought they knew all there was to know about gifts, but such was not
actually the case. They had limited the work of the Spirit to only a
few gifts. Today a great deal of ignorance exists concerning the matter of spiritual gifts because we have not been serious students of the
Scriptures to discover what God has to say on this matter.

This has been due in part to the lack of study material available on gifts until recent years. I grew up in the church, but I cannot remember being taught about spiritual gifts. It is fair to say that I may not always have paid sufficiently close attention, but the fact remains that it has not been a major topic in most mainline churches.

The second reason for our lack of understanding is the general apathy among many Christians for in-depth Bible study. I commend you for your diligence in working through this book out of your concern to know about gifts in general and about your gift specifically. I am confident that God will reward your persistent study.

Fear of the Unknown

"I'm not a charismatic?" "I don't want to talk about spiritual gifts, because I don't want to lose control." Such statements indicate a fear on the part of many when the discussion centers on issues concerning the Holy Spirit. A fear of spiritual gifts has come from the apparent abuse of spiritual gifts by some in the Christian community. It has emanated from the exaggerated emphasis on tongues and from the confusion and church splits that have often followed such teaching.

Gene Getz, a popular author, has himself discouraged gift discovery because of some of the dangers inherent in the gifts. He lists, for example, the confusion that has been produced in the church by false teaching on spiritual gifts. Further he points to the rationalization that sometimes occurs on the part of believers because of a misapplication of gift teaching. For example, some persons argue that they don't witness because they don't have the gift of evangelism. Finally, he points to self-deception that occurs among believers about their giftedness.[3]

These are all legitimate fears, and we could add others such as spiritual arrogance over one's gift. Another concern that I have has to do with the confusion between gifts and personality temperaments. I often hear people excuse their offensive behavior because of their spiritual gift. "I respond this way," they argue, "because I'm a prophet." Our gifts should not be used to excuse our intolerance or lack of concern for others. Paul always placed his discussion of gifts in the context of Christian love and unity.

While such fears of abuse and confusion are real, they should not deter us from seeking to discover and use our gifts for the good of the body. Paul, himself, confronted some of the same problems in

Corinth, yet he did not refuse to teach about gifts or hesitate to encourage the Corinthians to seek the higher gifts. The best way to counter fear and false teaching is through a diligent study of God's Word.

I trust that the earlier chapters of this book have helped to eliminate any fear that would prohibit you from seeking to discover your special gifts. You do not have to speak in tongues in order to be filled with the Spirit. You do not have to lose rational control in order to minister through your giftedness. Paul exhorted his readers to seek those gifts which were best suited for the edification of the church. I would encourage you to follow Paul's advice and ask God for those gifts which would enable you to best serve Him in your local church. You need not fear; your Father delights in giving good gifts.

The Fog Factor

I believe that the greatest deterrent for most laypeople has been the fog factor created, in part, by the recent proliferation of literature available on this subject. This may appear to contradict what was said in the preceding section, but such is not the case. Often the more you read on this topic, the more confused you become. Just how many gifts are there? Those holding to a traditional view have argued for nine gifts, but if you have read extensively on this topic you have discovered that other writers argue for eleven, fifteen, sixteen, twenty, or twenty-seven. Often the differences are accounted for because some list only those gifts occurring in a specific listing of gifts such as 1 Corinthians 12:28-29, while other writers include giftlike abilities found in the surrounding text such as hospitality, voluntary poverty, and others. A few writers include Old Testament passages and list gifts related to craftsmanship.

I think it is legitimate to include such abilities as craftsmanship and musical abilities although they are not included on a New Testament list. The mention of the Spirit and the language of Exodus 31:3-5 confirms such as conclusion. "And I have filled him with the Spirit of God in wisdom, in understanding, in knowledge, and in all kinds of craftsmanship, to make artistic designs for work in gold, in silver, and in bronze, and in the cutting of stones for settings, and in the carving of wood, that he may work in all kinds of craftsmanship." Musical ability is often mentioned in the Old Testament. New Testament passages such as 1 Corinthians 14:26 and Colossians 3:16 support the argument that musical abilities should be understood to be spiritual gifts. It is unimportant that musical abilities do not occur on any of the actual lists of gifts.

We must avoid the tendency to put the Holy Spirit in our little box and assert that He must work in a certain way or give a specified number of gifts. It doesn't matter whether our box is a charismatic box or an evangelical box, a box is a box. Just as the Holy Spirit was free to empower a craftsman for the needs of the tabernacle, or the apostles for the foundational work of the church, so He is free to give new gifts today according to the needs of the church. If a *primary purpose* of the gifts is to enable the believer to *function meaningfully* in the church for the fulfillment of the Great Commission, then we can conclude that the Holy Spirit will gift the church to fulfill this commission in every generation and in every situation. It should not surprise us that He would distribute new gifts as the opportunities of ministry require them or that some gifts may be discovered functioning in some churches and not in others. The Holy Spirit is free to give the gifts as He desires.

To avoid the confusion created by the various gift lists, I have chosen not to give any such list in this book. If you think such a list might prove helpful to you in discovering your own gift, then by all means use it. You can find a thorough description of the gifts compiled from the lists of the New Testament in Kenneth Gangel's book, *Unwrap Your Spiritual Gifts;* Rich Yohn's, *Discover Your Spiritual Gift and Use It;* or Jack MacGorman's, *The Gifts of the Spirit.*[4] Use these lists if you find them helpful, but do not limit the Holy Spirit's creative work in your life. You may discover that your gift does not appear on any list. Don't let that disturb you. As your reflection in the mirror is unique, so are your spiritual gifts. Just thank God for your unique gift and ask Him how you can use it in your local church.

One other question that has created a "fog of confusion for some" is the relationship between spiritual gifts and natural talents. Must our gift be a new and unique ability without any connection to the talents we brought with us into our Christian experience? Let's look briefly at that question before we go on to the discovery process.

Spiritual Gifts and Natural Talents

How are spiritual gifts related to natural talents? This question has been addressed by virtually everyone writing on spiritual gifts. Most

authors have argued for a radical discontinuity between gifts and talents.[5] They assert that gifts should not be seen as spiritually energized talents. I have always been interested in this question both in
terms of biblical revelation and actual practice. So let's explore this
together for a moment.

I believe that many persons have been kept from meaningful service because they have been led to believe that their spiritual gift
must be some ability that is totally new and completely discontinuous with their preconversion experience. Yet I have met very few
persons who give testimony to having received a new gift after conversion that is totally discontinuous with their preconversion experience and ability. If we set aside for the moment the more ecstatic
gifts such as tongues, this would be true nearly 100 percent of the
time. Remember that Paul had some difficulty with the use of the
ecstatic gifts in the assembly of believers.

To adequately explore this matter, we must answer the question
that Paul posed to the Corinthians: "What do you have that you did
not receive?" (1 Cor. 4:7) That question covers all of human life.
Who then is the author of our natural talents? Did we receive them
from Mother Nature? Of course not! God the Creator is the author of
our talents. He knit us together while we were still in our mother's
womb (Isa. 44:2). Can He not then use our talents in the context of
the church if He so chooses? Could it be that our talents, like our
physical bodies are transformed at the time of conversion so that they
can be used as instruments of righteous? I want to examine a few of
these questions before we proceed to the gift discovery section.

I agree with the authors who insist spiritual gifts are reserved only
for Christians. That goes without saying. I do not, however, think
that such a statement excludes the fact that talents and spiritual gifts
may be related. Further, I agree that spiritual gifts should not be seen
as "energized talents." I do however think that people may discover
that their spiritual gift lies in the area in which they were talented
prior to becoming a Christian. Their talents are not "souped-up,"
but rather "transformed" by the renewal of the Holy Spirit.

Scripturally, we could point to the similar transformation of the
human body. Look at Romans 6:12-13: "Therefore do not let sin
reign in your mortal body that you should obey its lusts, and do not
go on presenting the members of your body to sin as instruments of
unrighteousness; but present yourselves to God as those alive from
the dead, and your members as instruments of righteousness to
God." At birth we received our physical bodies as a gift from Cre-

ator God. Because of the spiritual blindness created by sin, we gave our bodies over to sin. We used the members of our body in selfish and sometimes sinful enterprises. When we became Christians and the scales of sin were removed from our eyes, we could then see that all of life was a gift of God. Because of the life-giving power of the Holy Spirit, we were empowered to give the members of our bodies to God for service to Him. The tongues and hands we now possess are the same tongues and hands that we possessed before our conversion, but with a radical difference—they have now been made alive by the Holy Spirit. They have been transformed! For that reason they can and must be given to Him in service.

It is significant that Paul began the gift passage in Romans 12:1-8 with the injunction: "I urge you therefore, brethren, by the mercies of God, to present your bodies a living and holy sacrifice, acceptable to God, which is your spiritual service of worship" (v. 1). The Christian must present his body with all that entails to God so that he may be of service to Him. Because of the transformation that occurs at conversion, the gift of our body is now acceptable to Him.

I believe that many persons have been kept from meaningful service because they have been led to believe that their spiritual gift must be some ability that is totally new.

Our spiritual gifts are nothing more than the abilities which enable us to serve God while in this physical body. Just as the Spirit of God transforms and energizes our physical body, I believe He transforms and energizes our talents in such a way that we can legitimately refer to them as spiritual gifts when properly understood and surrendered to His lordship.

Let's think through the process together. When you receive Jesus Christ, you are baptized by the Holy Spirit into the body of Christ. You become a spiritual person. One of the consequences of your new birth is the presence of the Holy Spirit, who enables you to know:

All that God has prepared for those who love Him. For to us God revealed them through the Spirit; for the Spirit searches all things, even the depths of God. For who among men knows the thoughts of a man except the spirit of the man, which is in him? Even so the thoughts of God no one knows except the Spirit of God. *Now we have received, not the spirit of the world, but the Spirit who is from God, that we might know the things freely given to us by God* (1 Cor. 2:9b-12, emphasis mine).

The Holy Spirit enables you to see that everything you possess is a gift of the grace of God—your life, your body, your gifts—everything. You are now able to present your body and your talents to Him for service. It is at this point of surrender for service that we receive the infilling of the Holy Spirit. It is the infilling that energizes all our gifts so that they become supernatural in effect. The command of Paul to be continually being filled with the Spirit (Eph. 5:18) was focused on being receptive to the constant empowering of the Holy Spirit to enable us to serve the Lord.

Let's look at an example. I recently spent some time with my good friend Harry Dent. Harry is a layman who has a gift for teaching the Word of God. I asked Harry, "Could you teach before you became a Christian?" He responded in the affirmative. Then I asked him about the difference in his teaching now and his teaching prior to his conversion. His answer was enlightening. He first mentioned the obvious difference in content. Second, he noted that people often told him that his teaching was a blessing and that they felt the presence of the Spirit. A third distinctive was his motivation to edify the body of Christ. A genuine spiritual gift will always have as its aim the edification of the body of Christ and thus the fulfillment of the Great Commission. This is an example of a talent for teaching transformed into a spiritual gift.

Christians must be receptive to the constant empowering of the Holy Spirit to enable them to serve the Lord.

We could think about a gifted pianist who attends church. This person sits under the teaching of God's Word and is converted. As he grows in understanding, he desires to serve the Lord through his church. He now understands that his ability to play the piano is a gift from God and wants to use this gift to edify the church. Should we not affirm this person in his giftedness and encourage him in his willingness to serve the body of Christ through his spiritual gift?

Jeremiah, the Old Testament prophet, declared that God had called him and appointed him a prophet while he was still in his mother's womb. From birth he possessed the gifts that God would energize by the Holy Spirit so that he could function as a prophet to the nations. In a different way Moses provides us with a picture of how God can utilize that which we already possess. The shepherd's staff which Moses threw to the ground in His encounter with God, became the rod of God when transformed by His might. A simple shepherd's staff became the mighty rod which was held out over the Red Sea. It was the rod held aloft during the battle with the Amalekites.

One can think of the apostle Paul, who as the chief of sinners, led others in persecuting Christians. Once saved, this man's powerful personality, tenacious spirit, and ability to move people to commitment were transformed by God to enable him to become the apostle to the Gentiles.

A couple words of balance and warning are necessary. First, this does not mean that God cannot give new gifts that have no connection with our previous talents. He can and He does. We cannot put the Holy Spirit in "the talent-transformation box" either. You should remain open to these new gifts of the Spirit. I believe that most persons, however, will discover their gifts among the talents given by God at birth. In my experience this has been the rule and not the exception. I do not want to be guilty, however, of causing you to limit the sovereign work of the Spirit. Thus I believe we are dealing with a both/and situation and not an either one/or the other situation. Spiritual gifts can be both new abilities given after conversion and talents possessed prior but transformed through conversion.

Let me try to illustrate this visually. In the chart on page 154 we can see why some ministry is not productive or meaningful. First, if a person is a church member and serving in the church but has never been born again, he is using natural talents in a supernatural endeavor (picture 2). This is the equivalent of using a water pistol in a showdown at the OK Corral. This will always create problems such as church dissension and personal frustration. For example, we might have a CPA who is an excellent accountant. He attends church and wants to be of some use to the church family. He becomes involved on the accounting committee and appears to be very useful. One evening the accounting committee encounters a problem that calls for the church to exercise faith as well as common sense. The man is perplexed and troubled because none of the discussion seems

Discovering Your Spiritual Gifts

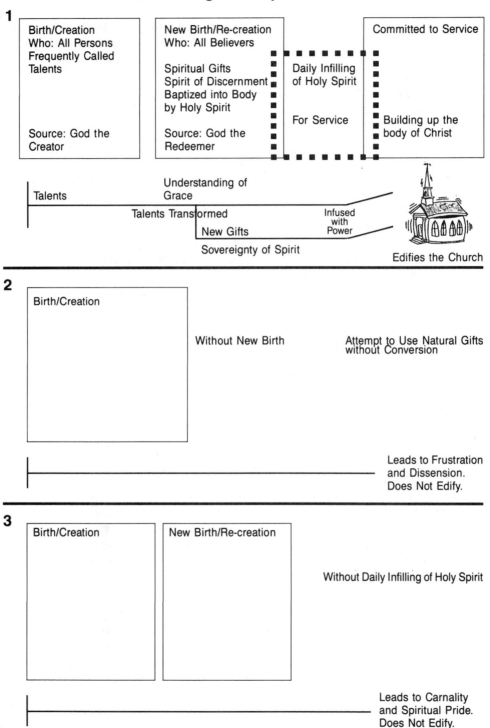

1

Birth/Creation
Who: All Persons
Frequently Called
Talents

Source: God the
Creator

New Birth/Re-creation
Who: All Believers

Spiritual Gifts
Spirit of Discernment
Baptized into Body
by Holy Spirit

Source: God the
Redeemer

Daily Infilling
of Holy Spirit

For Service

Committed to Service

Building up the
body of Christ

Talents

Understanding of
Grace

Talents Transformed

New Gifts

Sovereignty of Spirit

Infused
with
Power

Edifies the Church

2

Birth/Creation

Without New Birth

Attempt to Use Natural Gifts
without Conversion

Leads to Frustration
and Dissension.
Does Not Edify.

3

Birth/Creation

New Birth/Re-creation

Without Daily Infilling of Holy Spirit

Leads to Carnality
and Spiritual Pride.
Does Not Edify.

reasonable. He is still thinking with the natural mind. This may lead to an angry discussion, frustration within the committee, and ultimately dissension in the church. Natural talents without the transformation of the new birth will never be effective in service to the body. It is dangerous to give a ministry role to an individual who has not been converted.

Another scenario could depict the person who commits her life to Christ and comes to understand her spiritual gift, but then attempts to serve the body through that gift without the daily infilling of the Spirit (picture 3). The results will be carnality and spiritual arrogance. The use of the gift will not result in edification, but rather it will be fruitlessness service or, worse yet, dissension within the community. Corinth provides a clear example of a situation where gifts were being used in a carnal manner. The motivation of many of the spirituals in Corinth was to be seen or heard. The driving force behind the use of their gifts was pride not edification. For that reason Paul redefined the spiritual person in terms of love. The evidence of the infilling of the Holy Spirit is the manifestation of love in personal relationships and the supernatural empowering of the gifts for the edification of the church. It is therefore possible for gifted people to serve in the context of their giftedness in a carnal and unproductive manner. We must be careful that we are continually filled with the Spirit.

The Four Steps to Discovery

Many of the practical books on spiritual gifts will offer suggestions for discovering your gifts that are similar to these. That gives us some affirmation that we are on the proper path for discovery. I suggest four steps for the entire process—1) discern, 2) surrender/ empower, 3) develop, and 4) employ. The following discussion will clarify each step. We will look at the first two in this chapter and the final two in chapter 10. Let me encourage you not to rush through this section or this process. Be prepared to spend plenty of time in front of the mirror. Be patient, allow the Holy Spirit to reveal Himself to you, and in so doing He will make apparent your gift. Our greatest desire must always be to know God, not just to discover our gift.

Certain fundamentals exist that I have taken for granted up to this point. They are covered in the Bible study portion of this book, but for completeness, I will review them before we begin our gift discovery journey together. 1) You must be a Christian to discover your spiritual gift. Only believers can be gifted for service by God's Holy Spirit. Being a Christian doesn't mean belonging to a church, it means belonging to God. To become Christians we must be born again by the Spirit of God. To do that you must agree with God about your sin, be willing to turn from your sin, and accept Christ as your Savior. If you are not sure whether you have made such a decision, turn to appendix A and read that page. Further, I would suggest that you talk with your pastor or a Christian friend about your desire to be born again. 2) You must trust the Holy Spirit to give you good gifts. Don't approach this process with fear but with anticipation. 3) You must desire to know your gift. 4) You must be willing to use your gift in service to the body of Christ. This is a good time for a motivation check. Why do you want to discover your gift?

The Process of Discernment

Do you remember our discussion of 1 Corinthians 2:9-16? Look at those verses in your Bible. Paul began that section with an announcement of the wonderful things that God has prepared for those who love Him. The natural person cannot understand them, but they have been revealed to us through the Spirit. Look at verse 12: "Now we have received, not the spirit of the world, but the Spirit who is from God, that we might know the things freely given to us by God." God wants you to discover your gifts, and He alone can reveal them to you by the Holy Spirit. I'm going to give several practical suggestions in the following pages for discovering your gift, but I want to be clear and honest: only the Holy Spirit can reveal your giftedness.

In general I have not found gift surveys to be productive. First, I fear that they have been used as a shortcut, causing some Christians to avoid concerted prayer. Second, they may cause the user to overlook gifts not listed on a particular survey tool. A survey, by its very design, will select a given number of gifts. Third, surveys often cause the user to practice a subtle form of gift projection. It is usually not difficult to tell which gift, from a list of fourteen or fifteen, is being treated by a particular question. Therefore, if you desire a certain gift you can answer the questionnaire in such a manner to score highly in that particular area. I have found myself doing that on some of the personality inventories so popular today. I answer the questions, all the time, thinking about how I would like to respond or how I should act in a given situation. It is possible to take a gift inventory with one's mind already made up concerning giftedness only to discover that we score highly in the area of our *desire*, rather than our *actual giftedness*.

Only the Holy Spirit can reveal your giftedness.

On the other hand, some Christians have found the survey to be a helpful tool in the discernment process. A survey can work like an aptitude test administered by a guidance counselor. It can provide helpful suggestions. If you choose to use such a tool, approach it with prayer, answer honestly, and be willing to allow the Spirit to direct you to gifts that may lie beyond the parameters of that particular tool. Because I desire this book to be as useful as possible, I have included a list and description of several such surveys in appendix B. I would, however, encourage you to continue with this section before you turn to appendix B.

1. *Prayer is the key.*—James 4:2 tells us: "You do not have because you do not ask." Begin with the obvious step—ask God to reveal your special area of giftedness. Don't rush this process. Keep on asking, keep on seeking, keep on knocking, and claim the promise that He will answer and you will discover. I am disconcerted that many Christians would rather spend thirty minutes filling out a gift inventory than thirty minutes talking with their Father about their giftedness. If you have been asking, but still are unsure read James 4:3, "You ask and do not receive, because you ask with wrong motives, so that you may spend it on your pleasures." Be transparent in prayer. Your Father knows the very thoughts and intents of your mind and heart. Make sure that your motivation in discovering your gift is related to your passion to edify the body of Christ through the use of your gift and not to exalt yourself.

2. *Understanding your passion.*—What is your true passion? What would you do if all barriers were removed? I remember the first time I preached a message on spiritual gifts and talked about discovering your gifts through the understanding of your passion. A lady in our church caught me in the hallway after the service. She

questioned me, "Pastor, were you serious about that message?" "Yes," I replied, a little shakily. I wasn't exactly sure about the point of her question. "Good," she retorted, "I resign." Seeing my consternation, she laughed and told me the reason for her question and resignation. "I have been the head of the preschool for several years, but I have always had a desire to teach the handicapped. You just freed me up to do that. I'll finish out the church year in preschool but, with your blessing, I want to start a Sunday School class for the handicapped." She did just that and organized one of the first Sunday School classes in Virginia for the mentally handicapped. Our passion can help us to identify both our area of giftedness and the practical use of our gifts within the life of the church.

I am disconcerted that many Christians would rather spend thirty minutes filling out a gift inventory than thirty minutes talking with their Father about their giftedness.

3. *Where do you find fulfillment?*—Many Christians labor under a common misconception; "If I'm doing the will of God, I have to be miserable." I can remember that as a youth I was convinced that if I ever surrendered to God, He would assuredly send me to deepest and darkest Africa where I would have to live in a mud hut and eat rotten monkey meat. Obviously my overactive childhood imagination had been fueled by too many missionary slide presentations. Nonetheless, my fear was real and expressed the idea that serving God must be laborious or it isn't true service. Let's be perfectly honest, some of our work in any area is demanding, and some things we must do because we "ought" to do them. Yet our service to the Lord through our gifts should be fulfilling and invigorating. Many Christians experience burnout because they are attempting to serve in areas for which they are not gifted.

In my own ministry I know that I am energized by preaching. I enjoy everything about the preaching task. It is hard physical labor to do three morning worship services, and I am tired when finished, but I am also fulfilled because I am using my primary gift. Counseling for me is quite another matter. After about two hours of heart-wrenching counseling, I'm ready for the sauna. I am willing to do the counseling as a part of my pastoral ministry, but I serve more productively in my giftedness when I am preaching.

4. *Affirmation of others.*—Oftentimes the Holy Spirit will use the affirmation of other believers to assist you in discovering your gifts. As you pray, think about times when someone has told you that you ministered to them. It may have been when you sent them a note, took them a meal, or sang a solo. You might also want to think about times that your pastor or some mature Christian friend has affirmed a special ministry task or told you that you have a special gift for ministry. You could also seek the counsel of mature believers on this matter. Ask them what areas of giftedness they see in you. Once again I would caution you that even the counsel of godly friends must be confirmed by the Holy Spirit through prayer.

5. *Needs in the body of Christ.*—If we believe that God has placed us in the body just as He Himself chose, then one clue to our giftedness should be the ministry needs of our own church. In truth, this is the clearest indicator of giftedness. God's desire in the giving of the gifts is to build His body and not simply to exalt our ego. What area of need exists in your church that causes you concern? What one need keeps surfacing in your own prayer time? You might want to ask yourself what you see God doing in and through your church and commit to join Him in that activity. God generally distributes gifts in accord with His present activity. When we discover God's activity, we will have put ourselves in the proper position to discover our unique gifts. To discover your spiritual gift, simply watch to see what God does through you to edify His body, the church.

6. *Try several areas of service.*—If you find that after all the above steps you continue to come up blank, try several areas of service. Ray Steadman argues that we discover a spiritual gift just like we discover natural talents, by experimentation.[6] For example, you would not have known that you had an aptitude for cooking if you had never attempted to cook. You would not have discovered that you could ski without trying. Get involved in the life of your church at a point of need and seek confirmation from the Holy Spirit. Look at the results of your service: Are you effective in this area of ministry?[7] Have others affirmed you in what you are doing? Do you find fulfillment? Don't be discouraged if you don't hit upon your gift the first time. Every time you eliminate a gift that you don't have, you are coming one step closer to discovering the gift that you do have. Besides, you will be making new friends in the church and, most importantly, growing in your relationship with your Father.

Many Christians experience burnout because they are
attempting to serve in areas for which they are not gifted.

Surrender/Empower

How does the infilling of the Holy Spirit relate to the discovery and use of the spiritual gifts? That is a good question, but one which has not been adequately addressed.

You may have noticed that in the chart on page 154, I drew the box entitled "Daily Infilling of the Holy Spirit" so that it overlapped the "Conversion" box and the "Surrendered for Service" box. I did so to indicate two things. What it means to be filled with God's Spirit is understood by different persons at different times in their spiritual experience. One individual may not immediately appropriate the infilling of the Spirit simply because he or she is not taught to do so. In other cases, one may be afraid to surrender to the infilling of the Spirit because of some preconceived notion. Whatever the reason, the infilling may be understood and experienced at different moments by different individuals in the Christian walk.

Second, the infilling of the Spirit is not a once for all religious experience; it is a daily process. Look at Ephesians 5:18-19: "Be filled with the Spirit, speaking to one another in psalms and hymns and spiritual songs, singing and making melody with your heart to the Lord." The verb is present tense and could be rendered, "be continually being filled." I am not suggesting that God withholds anything from the believer at conversion, nor am I talking about a second event where God finally gives us the Spirit. The Holy Spirit is given at conversion. He convicts us and converts us. He initiates or baptizes us into the body (1 Cor. 12:13). *The terminology "baptism of the Holy Spirit" should be reserved for the discussion of conversion. The baptism of the Spirit describes the process whereby the Holy Spirit immerses us into the life of Christ and His body, the church*. Yet for many believers there is a further point of surrender to the Spirit, where we allow ourselves to be infilled for service. When you read the biographies of great Christian leaders you will find that all have this point of surrender in common. They may use different terminology to refer to their experience, but all alike have a point of reference where they surrendered themselves fully to the work of the Savior and were filled up with the Spirit. They began to walk in the Spirit and serve in the Spirit. I believe the infilling of the Holy Spirit is a must for any Christian who wants to utilize his or her gift for service in the Body of Christ.

Have you ever heard people talking about an individual preaching with "unction?" Have you heard persons refer to the music or worship service as being "anointed" or "empowered?" All of these expressions point to the use of gifts in full surrender to the Holy Spirit. This also explains why we can sometimes serve in the area of our giftedness and fall flat. If we are serving at any given moment without the full empowering of the Holy Spirit, even our gifted service will have little effect.

The infilling of the Spirit is not a once for all religious experience; it is a daily process.

Being filled with the Spirit is a daily process of surrender and appropriation. The Holy Spirit came to indwell us the moment we received Christ. We became the temple of the Holy Spirit. He indwells us as our new manager. He desires therefore to empower and control us, and as such He can keep the old nature at bay. Because our old nature wants to rule, we must daily agree with God about our sin (confess) and then volitionally turn from that sin (repent). This process allows God to cleanse us from all unrighteousness. We cannot be full of sin and the Holy Spirit at the same moment. Once we have thoroughly completed this step, we must present our body to our new manager (Rom. 6:13). This process should be repeated each morning and at any moment during the day when you discover that sin has separated you from the presence of the Father and the empowering of the Spirit.

Unless we are filled with the Spirit and walk daily in the Spirit, we will not function appropriately according to our gifts. We may find ourselves attempting to serve God from our own fleshly strength, which always produces frustration. Sometimes, in this carnal state, we are tempted to use our gifts for our own purposes rather than for the edification of the body. It is this constant infilling of the Spirit that provides the supernatural empowering for the effective use of our gifts and keeps us focused on their proper use in the body. The Holy Spirit produces both the fruit of the Spirit (Gal. 5:22-24) and empowers the gifts. For that reason it is essential that the believer always be full of the Spirit. The infilling will always ensure that the gifts are used in their proper context of love.

If you have never gone through the steps mentioned above to seek the infilling of the Holy Spirit, you should do that right now. 1. Ask the Holy Spirit to reveal all sin and then confess and repent. 2. Present your body to the Holy Spirit. Ask Him to fill and empower you for service. 3. Learn to listen to His voice as He guides you throughout the day and provides opportunity for service. Remember you are not seeking a mystical experience, but you are walking in obedience to God's Word.

Reflections in the Mirror

Our reflections section will be longer in this chapter because we will take a look at an open-ended gift survey to help in the discovery of our gifts. You are not to think that you must find your gift on some particular gift list. God is infinitely creative and is capable of granting new gifts for the work of ministry today. Many times our gifts lie latent below the surface of our consciousness and simply await discovery and development. Often people will discover that what they have considered to be only a natural talent is in truth the gift God gave to them even in their mother's womb. Through the process of conversion and infilling of the Spirit, these natural talents are infused by the Spirit and are rightly called spiritual gifts. As such, they must be placed under His lordship and used for service to the body. These gifts are just as supernatural as any gift given subsequent to conversion.

The constant infilling of the Spirit provides the supernatural empowering for the effective use of our gifts and keeps us focused on their proper use in the body.

You *could* fill out this survey in a matter of minutes if you choose to do so, *but I would warn against such a rushed procedure.* Please view this as a prayer guide. Remember to ask the Giver to reveal the area of your giftedness.

1. What do you do well that encourages other believers? ____
_____
_____

2. In what areas of service do you find the greatest satisfaction, fulfillment, and energy? _____
_____
_____

3. What ministry area generates for you the greatest sense of genuine enthusiasm and excitement? _____
_____
_____

4. List areas of service that you perform that cause people to say: "You really do that well. You ministered to me." _____
_____
_____

5. Has your pastor or other close, mature church member suggested areas of giftedness? What were they? _____
_____
_____

6. If there were no limitations, to what area of ministry in your church would you be most inclined? _____
_____
_____

7. Have you sought any training to develop your gifts? Remember the pastor/teacher is to equip the saints for the work of ministry.

What training provided the greatest stimulation and created the most interest? _____
_____
_____

8. Are you willing to be trained? _____
9. List the areas of service you have attempted where you did not feel fulfilled or encouraged. _____
_____
_____
_____

10. Do you discern needs in the church that aren't being met and that cause you great concern? Which ones cause you the greatest concern?_____

_____

_____

11. Have you been praying for a particular area of the church's ministry? _____ What area? _____

_____

_____

12. What abilities or talents do you have that could be leading you to service in these ministries? _____

_____

_____

_____

    a. Are you willing to surrender them to the lordship of Christ right now and allow Him to full empower them for His service?

    _____

    b. Would you be willing to allow your pastor to provide or suggest further training in this area? _____

    c. Will you use it for the edification of the body? _____

If you had difficulty listing abilities or talents:

    a. Ask the Holy Spirit to give you the ability you desire to meet the unique need that has burdened you.

    b. Share with your pastor and another mature friend this desire and ask them to pray with you.

    c. Ask your pastor if training is available to help you to develop the gift you are seeking.

    d. Commit now to use your gift(s) solely for God's glory in service to His body.

Remember These Five Keys

1) *Seek spiritual discernment.*—Spiritual gifts can be abilities given by God before conversion that are now recognized and submitted to Him, or they can be new abilities given to meet specific needs in your church. Remember that we have received the Spirit of God; "that we might know the things freely given to use by God" (1 Cor. 2:12). Ask God to reveal your gift(s) for ministry.

2) *Be willing to submit your gift(s) to the Lordship of Christ.*—When you commit your gift to His lordship, it is His to do with as He wills. You serve then at His direction and not your convenience. Bring your gift under the authority of your church's leadership. This will provide the body's validation and confirmation.

3) *Use your gift in the context of the body of Christ.*—All gifts are given for the common good. Ask your church leadership to help you become involved in the ministries of the church. If your particular gift creates an area of ministry in the broader community, it should still function in the context of the church. For example, persons with the gift of evangelism might function in a broader sphere than one local church, but they should still be accountable to the church and focus the results of their work on the edification of the body.

4) *Seek to abound for the good of the body.*—You can joyously seek spiritual gifts if your motives are pure and you can abound for the good of the body.

5) *Remain open to training.*—Remain open to training for the full development of your gifts to the glory of God. God has gifted the pastor to equip the saints for the work of ministry.

What Now?

Now that you have completed the chapter on discovering your gift(s), you may be wondering what you must do next. Some of you may be thinking that nothing has happened. If you were expecting some overwhelming ecstatic experience, you may feel disappointed. I have discovered that ecstatic experiences do occur in the spiritual life, but they are given by God's sovereign design and usually have little to do with our giftedness for service.

If you are still unsure of your gift, don't despair. Keep on knocking, keep on seeking, and keep on asking. The Father desires to give you good gifts. While you are praying about this matter, learn to focus on your fellowship with the Father. Sometimes we discover something more quickly when our focus is elsewhere.

You can also begin immediately with the experimentation process mentioned above. See your pastor and ask him where you might serve in the church family. As you serve, ask God for specific direction. "Lord is this an area of ministry to which you are calling me?" Don't forget to continue to walk in the Spirit daily.

You may be sort of frustrated—you've closely evaluated all the gifts, such as prophecy, teaching, administration, etc. that Paul mentioned in his writings, but you still cannot seem to put your finger on the type of gift to which the Lord is calling you. Let's look past the reflections from the shore and take a boat ride on the river. See if the Lord shows you a reflective glimmer.

Spiritual gifts can be abilities given by God before conversion that are now recognized and submitted to Him, or they can be new abilities given to meet specific needs in our church.

Are you one of those people to which others say, "You have a nack for making everyone feel at home" or "We are always so comfortable around you." Maybe your area of giftedness would include being a greeter in your Sunday School class or in the lobby or entrance of your church. Or maybe that relaxing smile is just what a nervous visitor needs while trying to find a parking space for the first time in your church parking lot!

We have already established that God, our Creator, can transform our natural talents into spiritual gifts of service. How about those of you, then, who have abilities such as sewing? Maybe your gift includes helping with costumes for Christmas/Easter programs. For you artistic types, how about set design or decorating the lobby or your classroom bulletin board? And what is available for the technically minded? Have you ever tried running a sound board or monitoring a tape or helping with the audio system?

Do you really enjoy working with children? There is probably no church in existence that couldn't use help with preschool or youth! Or maybe you would like to organize some individuals who could take care of the children of single parents during special events.

But you say, "I'm an idea person. I can think of creative solutions, but I'm not good with the specifics." That's why God gifted the body with diversity. If you are an idea person, then undoubtedly there will be a down-to-earth, do-it person just waiting to dig in to the practical side of your creativity. Ask God to bring those detail-oriented individuals to your attention. Our church provides weekly sessions for adult Sunday School teachers. They are led by educators/fellow teachers who go over the next week's lesson and then provide innovative and thought-provoking ideas on how the material can be presented. Those who have the gift of teaching are often looking for better ways to get the point across.

Do you see a need in your church that you feel could be addressed but no one has ever done it before? Maybe the Lord is laying on your heart to be a pioneer of sorts. I mentioned earlier about the woman who stepped out of the realm of traditional service to start a program for the handicapped. What burden has the Lord brought to your mind?

You may not feel comfortable with everyone in conversation, but you love to express yourself on paper. Maybe you can help with your church newsletter—or start one! Maybe you belong to a church which keeps costs down by using volunteers to clean. You may have "the patience of a saint" that it takes to routinely vacuum or clean those pews.

Are you one of those who has a list for everything? Your gift could be used in the area of Sunday School records. Not everyone can keep an accurate count of class members while juggling visitor slips! How about all you shower singers? Have you considered the choir? But you're not a soloist, you say? Well, have you ever heard a choir full of soloists?! There may be more of a need there than you think.

The river of possibilities is endless. These are just a few ways you can use your gifts for His service. And do not fear. God has given you His lifejacket of assurance that every believer is gifted, and if you use His lifeline of prayer, He will not let you drown in your search.

Some of you have had the wonderful joy of receiving God's confirmation concerning your gift. Now you must employ that gift for the good of the body. God never gives His gifts for our amusement, but for the edification of the body. Plug in!

Whatever your present standing in this lifelong process of discovering and using your gifts, this next chapter should be an encouragement to you as we discover how we may develop our gifts and use them for the glory of the Lord.

Notes

1. C. Peter Wagner, *Your Spiritual Gifts Can Help Your Church Grow* (Regal Books: Calif., 1974).

2. Tract is available from Campus Crusade for Christ, Arrowhead Springs, San Bernardino, California.

3. Gene Getz, *Building One Another Up* (Wheaton, Ill.: Victor Books, 1976), 12-14.

4. Kenneth O. Gangel, *Unwrap Your Spiritual Gifts* (Wheaton, Ill.: Victor Books, 1983); Rick Yohn, *Discover Your Spiritual Gift and Use It,* (Wheaton, Ill.: Tyndale House, 1974); and Jack W. MacGorman, *The Gifts of the Spirit,* (Nashville, Broadman Press, 1974.

5. Peter Wagner, for example, argues that there is a radical discontinuity between gifts and talents. He insists that they are not "souped-up" talents. Wagner, 86-87.

6. Ray Steadman, *Body Life* (Glendale: Regal Books, 1972), 54.

7. Peter Wagner has an excellent section on experimenting with gifts and underlines the emphasis on effectiveness. Wagner, 116-26.

What You See Is
What You Give

"What you see is what you *get!*" How often have you heard that line in your lifetime? Sometimes it is used in self-defense. "I am who I am and I am not about to change for anybody. I like the way I am." End of discussion.

If we change that phrase to read, "What you see is what you give," we will discover a more important truth. When you look into the mirror in the morning and notice the bags under the eyes, the wrinkles that weren't so obvious last time you looked, and the blood vessels that look like road maps in the white of your eyes, how well do you perform during that day? Or, even less dramatic, I can remember that as a teen I could look in the mirror and spot a developing pimple. My day was ruined. I was devastated, and I had little to give that day because of what I saw in the mirror.

Through this study we have discovered how important we are to God. We have found that He is our strength and security. Through the Holy Spirit, we have been empowered to carry out His purpose and to contribute meaningfully to His body. We know that we belong and that our inherent worth is to be found in Him. He made us, redeemed us, gifted us, and placed us in the body just as He chose. This may be an entirely new reflected image for you. It is important that you learn to see yourself as God sees you because, "What you see is what you give!"

Consider this scenario. Bill has gazed intently into the perfect mirror of God's Word. He has had to clear away some of the false perceptions and negative images that he has been carrying from childhood. He has looked at himself under God's microscope and has begun to see his real beauty. He has carefully and prayerfully worked through the gift inventory. He has discovered that he has a gift for teaching and a real burden for the youth in the community. He has sought and received confirmation for these findings from his pastor and other mature Christian friends who know him well. From his new image Bill knows he has gifts worth giving. What now? Where does Bill go from here? What does he do with this newly discovered information?

The answer may seem obvious, and you might readily respond, "Give the guy a Sunday School class to teach." But let's use Bill's situation as a starting place. Do we simply give him a class? Not very likely, unless we're really struggling for teachers and the only qualifications are a beating heart and a willing spirit. We would anticipate that Bill would benefit from some training before we unleash him with his newly discovered gift. We would want to ensure that he employ his gift with the right focus and motivation. We want to be sure that Bill is spiritually prepared to enter the arena of active Christian service, and that he has some theological competence to accompany his gift of teaching. Thus we come to the last two steps of using spiritual gifts—the development and employment of the gifts.

Through this study we have discovered how important we are to God. We have found that He is our strength and security. He made us, redeemed us, gifted us, and placed us in the body just as He chose.

Developing Your Gifts

Some people apparently see a contradiction between spiritual gifts and training or development. They interpret using gifts as a spiritual activity and training as a human convention. This is not altogether different than the conviction of a past generation that theological education was a worldly contrivance that thwarted the work of the Spirit. Those who feared theological education or even sermon preparation would argue that they depended on the Spirit to give them what to say when they stood to preach or teach. It was as if they were saying that the Spirit could not work in the seminary setting or in the study. We have pretty well conquered that prejudice, but a similar one still exists in the area of spiritual gifts. The possession of a spiritual gift does not mean that an individual should eschew training prior to and during service.

On the flip side, I would hasten to say that all the training the church or the seminary has to offer cannot compensate for the absence of a particular gift. Therefore it is expedient that the church help members discover their gifts and serve in the area of their strongest gift.

Twice in the Pastoral Epistles, Paul exhorted Timothy to develop the spiritual gift which was in him. In 1 Timothy 4:14-15 Paul encouraged Timothy not to neglect the gift within him. Apparently his gift could atrophy through neglect. In order to stir his gift up, Paul said: "Take pains with these things; be absorbed in them, so that your progress may be evident to all" (v. 15). Timothy's growth in his gifted area would be obvious to those who observed his ministry.

In his second letter to young Timothy, Paul wrote, "And for this reason I remind you to kindle afresh the gift of God which is in you through the laying on of my hands" (1:6). He followed this reminder with an emphasis on the power, love, and discipline given to Timothy. God has given us the resources to bring our gifts to full power through discipline and development.

It is important that you learn to see yourself as God sees you because, "What you see is what you give!"

Biblically, we find the same joining of gifts and training in Ephesians 4:11-16 where Paul discussed the work of the pastor/teacher in equipping the saints for the work of ministry. Earlier in this same passage (v. 7), Paul affirmed that all believers had received a grace gift. In verse 16 he argued that the growth of the body depended upon the proper functioning of every member of the body. If we are to serve at peak efficiency, we must ban the idea that training is unspiritual or that gifts cannot be developed. The biblical model of church organization is neither a dictatorship nor a democracy, but a gifted body directed by God's gifted pastor/teacher who equips, coaches, and directs others in the full utilization of their gifts.

Gifts Are Developed by Training

If we go back to Bill, we would suggest that his first step after gift discovery would be to seek training so that he might be the most effective teacher possible. The church that is serious about involving the laity in ministry must be committed to quality training in order to enable church members to fully develop their spiritual gifts. The training format for Bill is fairly obvious. Most churches provide training for their teachers. There are plenty of good materials on the market that cater to this particular need. But how do we provide training for other areas of potential giftedness? This question has not been fully addressed because few churches have provided help in the area of gift discovery and, even those who have moved in this direction, have not given full consideration to the equipping program to support the gift discovery.

> *God has given us the resources to bring our gifts to full power through discipline and development.*

Let me give a few examples of the types of training the church might want to consider. Our church offers programs for training in the area of audio and video for those who are gifted and have a passion for such a ministry. We provide equipping for those who are gifted to serve through the music ministry. We have a twelve-week training course for those who serve the church through our deacon ministry. We have numerous levels of evangelism training functioning in the life of our church. Through these we are attempting to help people determine whether they have the gift of evangelism. Many other churches have similar training programs already in place, but they do not relate them to the individuals' area of giftedness. We must begin to think creatively about providing training for those who have the gift of mercy and want to express that gift through the ministries of their local church. I cannot list every area of potential giftedness and the corollary program that would support it, but I think you get the idea. The church that is serious about helping people fully utilize their gifts must be committed to develop the necessary training programs.

Gifts Are Developed Through Use

A spiritual gift is similar to a muscle in that it can be developed through use. Remember Paul encouraged Timothy not to neglect the gift in him, but to be absorbed in developing it. We have long recognized the principle of development through use. The gifted young pastor becomes more skilled at his pastoral task through on-the-job experience. We have all sat under the teaching of new Sunday School teachers who struggled through their first year of ministry only to become very accomplished teachers in time.

The local church must provide opportunities for developing spiritual gifts through use. The only dilemma this poses for the church is the spiritual care and nurture of the membership while the individual concerned is developing his or her gift. Some churches have made a beginning by providing programs like the youth week. During that week the youth are allowed to teach classes, lead the choir, and other such tasks. This has worked well in churches where mature leaders work with the inexperienced youth, coaching them in the tasks to be performed. The key to a successful youth week is the individual and personalized instruction from a mature leader, plus the opportunity for on-the-job training. Yet this program has some obvious defects. It lasts for only one week. It does not offer the opportunity for the entire membership to be involved.

The church that is serious about helping people fully utilize their gifts must be committed to develop the necessary training programs.

I mention the youth week only to point to a possible prototype for a training program based on use. We must seek to develop in-service training for the development of spiritual gifts. I had the privilege of serving on the staff with Mark Corts in Winston-Salem while I was attending Wake Forest. Mark took me with him on numerous ministry experiences. I look back on those days of ministry training and still find them to be some of the most valuable educational opportunities I had for developing my pastoral gifts. I didn't realize it at the time but I was receiving on-the-job gift development. We have developed an intern program for college and seminary students who have been called to full-time ministry. Through this program our church has worked hand in hand with the seminary in providing on-the-job training.

The on-the-job training principle is incorporated in programs like

Evangelism Explosion and *Continuous Witness Training,* but we have not applied this on-the-job training principle to other areas of gifted ministry. Why not enlist teachers to serve as trainees for several months? Provide opportunities for candidates for diaconate ministry to serve alongside deacons already in service. I should think that we could apply this principle to any area of gifted ministry.

Gifts Are Developed by Spiritual Discipline

Since gifts for ministry are spiritual in nature, it stands to reason that they will be enhanced as the believer grows in his/her walk with Christ. The gift of God to the believer is the Holy Spirit, and gifts for ministry are the expression of His infilling presence. Therefore when we grow in the knowledge of the Son's presence and power, we will see a corresponding growth in effectiveness in the employment of our gifts.

Paul's spiritual quest was defined by his desire to, ". . . know Him, and the power of His resurrection and the fellowship of His sufferings" (Phil. 3:10). Our goal is not simply to discover our gifts or to develop our gifts to their maximum effectiveness; *it is to know Christ.* As we grow in our relationship to Christ we will grow in our ability to employ our gifts for the good of the body of Christ. Our desire to unselfishly use our gifts for edification will be purified and our gifts fully energized as we learn to walk in the Spirit.

Many gifted Christians experience limited effectiveness because they neglect the basic spiritual disciplines. I know that my spiritual condition is revealed through using of my preaching gift. If I neglect the basic disciplines such as personal Bible study, prayer, and meditation, my preaching becomes less effective. I can study more, deliver my message with greater dramatic fervor, and none of these tactics will compensate for my lack of spiritual empowering. The same is true for any believer. Think for a moment about your most effective ministry encounters. Did they not come from the overflow of your personal relationship with God?

We must learn to walk in the constant empowering of the Holy Spirit. The gifted Christian needs to have a regular and consistent personal Bible study. We should follow Paul's direction to pray without ceasing. A quality prayer life is essential for the effective utilization of your spiritual gift. Without prayer we will soon become dry and lifeless. In order to develop our gifts fully we must walk in accountability to the body of Christ. We need the corporate experience of worship and fellowship. Through the body of Christ we expose ourselves to the gifts and ministry of others who will help us to continue to grow in our Christian walk and who can bring reproof and correction when necessary.

Our goal is not simply to discover our gifts or to develop our gifts to their maximum effectiveness; it is to know Christ.

Employing Your Gifts

The final step is the effective employment of the spiritual gifts for the good of the body of Christ. The spiritual gifts are practical, functional, and congregational; and therefore we cannot complete our discussion of the gifts until we consider their use.

Gifts Are Employed to Serve Others

Gifts are never given for our spiritual amusement, but for the edification of the body of Christ. The gifts are an expression of God's grace given by the exalted Christ to equip His children to build up His body, the church. The gifts provide the supernatural ability to enable us to work in a spiritual context to eternal ends. They enable us to care for one another in the body of Christ. In 1 Corinthians 12:25 Paul declared that the gifts have been given so "that the members should have the same care for one another." This, in turn, provides for and maintains the unity of the body. Unity is essential for the operation of the gifts, and the proper functioning of the gifts ensures the unity of the body.

Where gifts are properly employed, caring ministry and church unity will be clearly evidenced. A fully functioning New Testament church will be a "no-need" church. All the needs of the body will be met through the ministry of the diversely gifted members. We see a New Testament example in Acts 2:44-45: "And all those who had believed were together, and had all things in common; and they began selling their property and possessions, and were sharing them with all, as anyone might have need." Every need of the community was met through the gifted membership.

Gifts Are Employed for the Ministry of the Body

Spiritual gifts enable the local church to minister to its community. Every church is called to fulfill the Great Commission in ministering to its community, but not every church will employ the same strategy to reach its community. For this reason, the gift makeup of one church may be different from the gift makeup of another church. For example, one church may feel led to focus on reaching the singles in the community. Another church may feel a burden for those pregnant out of wedlock and concentrate on developing a crisis pregnancy center. In those cases, the Spirit of God will give those churches a different gift mix based on their ministry focus. We must believe that 1 Corinthians 12:18 is both true and practical. "But now God has placed the members, each one of them, in the body, just as He desired."

The gifts provide the supernatural ability to enable us to work in a spiritual context to eternal ends.

The sensitive church will first attempt to determine its gift mix before it defines its particular approach in fulfilling the Great Commission. If we remembered this truth, it would also help us to be more tolerant of churches in our community that do things somewhat differently than we do. If there is diversity within the local church, why do we insist on sameness within the broader body of Christ? A clearer understanding of the sovereign activity of the Spirit in the giving of gifts would enable local churches to fulfill their unique God-given task without feeling that they must offer all the ministries offered by a sister church. It would also encourage local churches to be more cooperative and less competitive.

Churches of the future will design their ministry and strategy based on an understanding of their God-given gift mix rather than on a traditional or even denominational program orientation. We have, in the past, been more committed to running our programs than ministering to our community by virtue of our church's unique giftedness. This means, of course, that the local church will need to help members discover, develop, and employ their gifts through the church. It means that the church will need to spend more time in prayer so that it can be sensitive to the leading of the Holy Spirit for its unique ministry. It means that we will of necessity be more cooperative with other like-minded churches who offer ministries different than our own. While these may be frightening observations to some traditionalists, I think they are exciting and challenging as we follow the prompting of the Holy Spirit.

Once again, we are led to the conclusion that the priority of the church is to determine the present activity of God and cooperate with Him in that which He is doing in their community. Understanding the activity of God is the clearest indicator of where the church must focus its ministry and therefore how God is gifting His church. Remember the basic understanding of "grace gifts" is that they are God's sovereign and unique gifting of His body, the church, to accomplish its mission in its sphere of influence and responsibility.

The sensitive church will first attempt to determine its gift mix before it defines its particular approach in fulfilling the Great Commission.

Gifts Are to be Employed Under the Authority of the Local Church

Since gifts are given for the good of the body, they must be used under the authority of the local church. The abuse of gifts in the Corinthian church had produced spiritual arrogance and had actually been destructive to the unity and ministry of the church. Paul placed guidelines on the use of the gifts in order to ensure that they were properly used for building up the body. He anticipated that some of the "spirituals" might be reluctant to accept any external authority concerning the use of their gifts. Thus he ended his extended gift discussion with the somber warning: "But if anyone does not recognize this [teaching], he is not recognized" (1 Cor. 14:38).

I think that we find another example of the use of the gifts under the authority of the local church in 1 Timothy 4:14; "Do not neglect the spiritual gift within you, which was bestowed upon you through prophetic utterance with the laying on of hands by the presbytery." Three points are worthy of note in this passage. 1) Timothy was qualified to lead the church at Ephesus by virtue of the gift within him. 2) This gift, apparently for pastoral leadership, had then been affirmed by another gifted leader who possessed the gift of prophecy. 3) Finally, Timothy functioned under the recognition and authorization of the presbytery (elders).[1]

The laying on of hands was the recognition and authorization of a gift rather than the bestowal of the gift. Gifts are sovereignly given by the Holy Spirit and are not dispensed through human hands. This passage gives us a help for understanding the modern-day practice of ordination. When the local church ordains individuals to the gospel ministry, that church affirms the candidates in their understanding of their gifts and calling to ministry. The persons, in turn, express their willingness to submit their ministry to the authority of the local church. Presently, most churches practice ordination only in the case of ministers and deacons. Perhaps we should rethink this practice in light of the biblical emphasis on spiritual gifts and shared ministry. Should we not have some service of recognition for all God's gifted servants, recognizing their unique gift and authorizing them to serve?

Placing gifts under the authority of the local church will ensure that the gifts are used to edify the body rather than glorify the individual. The authority of the local church provides checkpoints, balance, and accountability. Even those who exercise gifts whose impact may be broader than a specific local church need to minister under the authority and covering of a local church. For example, the person gifted in evangelism may be led to a crusade ministry which would provide a ministry field much larger than his own community. Yet, this gifted individual needs a connection to the body for the proper functioning of his gift. First, the results of his work must be sustained by the local work. Second, the gifted servant depends upon the other gifted members of the church to minister to him or her. It has been tragic to see that some gifted servants have attempted to serve in the broader ministry without integral connection to the body. Long-term results of such a ministry are often minimal and personal accountability is lacking. The hand severed from the body has no life in itself.

I have had the privilege of seeing this principle of gifts used under the authority of the local church at work in the ministry of Shelia Walsh and her husband Normal Miller. God has given Shelia a national ministry through her music and her gift to encourage believers. When I first met Shelia, I was impressed by her obvious gifts, but I was more impressed by her humility and balance. She expressed to me their desire to share in the ministry of the local church. They recognize their need to have a body of believers by whom they could be held accountable. They also understand the need to relate those to whom they minister to a local church for care. Their gifts are rightly related to the body.

Those whose gifts lead to ministry beyond the local church must stand under the authority of the church. If not, their effectiveness will be limited and their chance of personal and ministerial disaster will be greatly increased.

If we keep the context of the church always in view, it will lead us in finding and using our spiritual gifts. We will seek those gifts which provide the greatest opportunity for building up the body of Christ (1 Cor. 14:2), and we will employ them with due consideration to building up the body. This should put an end to the "free-agent" status of those who seek to exercise gifts apart from the authority of the local church. Many churches have struggled with the individual who starts a cell group without the support or knowledge of the church leadership. Such an unauthorized use of gifts has often led to church splits rather than the edification of the body. I have known of churches where persons attempted to exercise gifts of healing or deliverance without the knowledge of the pastor or other persons in positions of leadership. Such a practice is unbiblical and always leads to dissension.

Spiritual Gifts and Spiritual Warfare

Spiritual warfare is a topic seldom covered in books on spiritual gifts. Christians enter the arena of spiritual warfare the moment they become born-again believers. Paul reminded the Ephesians: "For our struggle is not against flesh and blood, but against the rulers, against the powers, against the world forces of this darkness, against the spiritual forces of wickedness in the heavenly places" (6:12). Yet the warfare becomes more intense the moment we begin to serve the Lord effectively through our spiritual gifts. In a sense we become a greater threat to Satan once we understand our giftedness and make a commitment to service. For example, Paul insisted that the pastor should not be a new convert lest through pride he fall prey to the devil (1 Tim. 3:6-7). The pastor, because of his ministry, becomes a prime target for the Adversary. Satan will often use a pastor's success to tempt him to pride so as to defeat him and render him ineffective for ministry. When a pastor falls prey to Satan's schemes, it has a disastrous impact on the ministry of the church.

I have long believed that one of the greatest dangers of the "charismatic" movement is the penchant for encouraging new Christians to seek tongues. This particular gift is such that it renders the mind unfruitful (1 Cor. 14:14). In this ecstatic state the naive young believer is more open to demonic influence. The new believer is frequently unprepared for such attack and becomes an early and unnecessary casualty in the spiritual conflict. Noncharismatic churches face a similar danger when they enlist new Christians for ministry tasks without any instruction on spiritual warfare. This may help us account for the rapid burnout of many new believers who are thrust into ministry without adequate preparation.

Much has been written recently about spiritual warfare. The church seems to be struggling for balance on this matter. For years we paid little attention to the reality of spiritual warfare, and now we may well be in danger of overemphasizing it in some quarters of the church. For that reason I will not attempt any exhaustive treatment of spiritual warfare other than summarize five principles believers need to know to serve effectively without falling prey to the enemy.

Focus on the Victor Rather than the Vanquished

As Christians our focus is to be on Christ and not on Satan. Many of the recent books on spiritual warfare spend too much time focusing on the Adversary, rather than encouraging Christians to appropriate their victory in Christ. If we are not careful we can unwittingly draw too much attention to the enemy. Recently a godly missionary, Nellie Pavluk, shared with our church about her mission experiences. Her work has placed her in dangerous and ungodly situations. After her presentation, someone asked her if she had seen a lot of demonic activity. Her answer was simple but profound. She stated that she did not think about Satan or look for his activity; she focused on Christ and His activity. That's good advice for all of us!

The government trains people to discover counterfeit bills by requiring them to spend days studying the real thing. By constantly handling the genuine article, the counterfeit becomes obvious to the touch. Do not put your focus on the Adversary; keep your focus on the Lord. James's advice should be heeded by all. "Submit therefore to God. Resist the devil and he will flee from you" (Jas. 4:7). The first step in the spiritual battle is to submit to God.

Be Assured That Spiritual Warfare Is Real

We must take the Bible seriously on this matter. Satan is real and he desires to destroy the work of the church. Paul's description of the Adversary and the armor of the believer in Ephesians 6 was not just intended for effect; it was intended for our instruction so that we might be thoroughly equipped for every good work. Peter warned the brethren: "Be of sober spirit, be on the alert. Your adversary, the devil, prowls about like a roaring lion, seeking someone to devour" (1 Pet. 5:8).

Be Aware of the Schemes of the Devil

The devil works through deception and temptation. He attacks us through the thought processes. For this reason Paul instructed the Corinthians to take every thought into captivity (2 Cor. 10:3-5). Further Paul speaks of the devil setting a snare for the unsuspecting believer (2 Tim. 2:26). Satan works his schemes by attacking us in the mind, the will, the emotions, and the flesh. Thus he can work through anger (Eph. 4:27), pride (1 Tim. 3:6-7), and other emotions to tear down the work of the church. He can tempt us to sins of the flesh which render our ministry ineffective. His battle is with the Lord, and Satan desires to render Christ's body, the church, ineffective by disabling and discrediting its gifted members.

Be Prepared

Don't be surprised by the attacks of the Adversary, but rather be prepared. *First,* to be thoroughly equipped we must continually be being filled with the Holy Spirit. Andy Anderson gave me a mental picture that has helped me with the appropriation of the infilling of the Spirit. The first thing in the morning imagine your body's like an empty shell filled with a murky liquid. To appropriate the infilling of the Spirit, you must first drain yourself of all sin. Start at the very top of your body with the mind and confess any sinful thought. As you confess those thoughts see that murky liquid dropping like mercury. Next confess any areas of sinfulness prompted by sight. Perhaps the

Holy Spirit will bring to mind the lustful or envious look. Next think of the ears and any participation you might have had in listening to rumor or gossip, etc. Continue with the mouth, arms, legs, and so on until you have fully confessed your sins.

Having fully confessed your sins, you are ready now to appropriate the infilling of the Holy Spirit. Invite the Holy Spirit to fill your body in the same manner you confessed your sins. For example, you might pray that the Holy Spirit would fill your tongue so that you would speak only those things which He would prompt you to say. As you pray for the infilling of your body, picture your body being filled with a crystal blue liquid representing the Holy Spirit.

Second, you must put on the full armor of God. The armor is well described in Ephesians 6:10-19. Again, I recommend that you actually visualize the armor as you prepare yourself for the day at hand. For example, pick up the breastplate of righteousness and strap it to your chest through prayer. Take each piece, in turn, and appropriate it through specific prayer. Thus armed, you are prepared to stand in God's victory.

We are not told to do battle with Satan. We are told to resist Satan and to stand victoriously in Christ's victory. I am uncomfortable with much of the teaching that encourages Christians to "rebuke" or "bind" Satan. We are not binding Satan. Christ has defeated Satan and we must submit to Christ so that we can stand in His victory. I find no biblical examples where believers are commanded to speak to or rebuke the Adversary Not even the archangel Michael dared pronounce judgment against the devil (Jude 9). Concentrate your focus on the Lord and allow Him to deal with the enemy.

Third, we must stand with the whole army of God. Not even the best-equipped soldier would be foolish enough to go to battle alone. We are not to stand alone against the Adversary, we are to stand with the whole army of God. Once again, we notice the importance of the fellowship of the body of believers. We are a dependent and interdependent people. We are totally dependent upon the Spirit for empowering, and we are interdependent in the life of the body since we are all members of one another.

Always Appropriate the Infilling of the Holy Spirit

I've already mentioned the importance of the infilling of the Holy Spirit, but I want to underline the supernatural work of the Spirit. When we attempt to serve, even in our gifted area, without the infilling of the Spirit, we are guilty of carnality. We cannot do supernatural work in fleshly power. If we do we will see an immediate drop-off in effectiveness. We will grow weary in our service and become discouraged easily. Drop out and apathy is the next logical step. This carnal state also makes us more vulnerable to spiritual attack.

The Effects of Gifts Properly Employed

In Ephesians 4:12-16 Paul elaborated on the value of gifts properly employed. He listed such practical concerns as edification, unity of the faith, spiritual maturity, doctrinal integrity, honest communication, and church growth. The end result of the proper use of spiritual gifts will be the growth of the church with the ultimate goal that: "we are to grow up in all aspects into Him, who is the head, even Christ, from whom the whole body, being fitted and held together by that which every joint supplies, according to the proper working of each individual part, causes the growth of the body for the building up of itself in love" (vv. 15-16).

In this book we've looked at gifts from both the biblical and the practical vantage points. We've discussed their significance to the individual and to his or her local church. By way of conclusion, let's take a moment to remind ourselves of the critical significance of spiritual gifts.

Reflections in the Mirror

1) *The gifts, properly employed, enable the church to fulfill the Great Commission.*—Because the work of the church is eternal in nature, this is by far the most important effect of the use of gifts. All other values must be seen as subordinate to this one. The gifts are the means whereby sovereign God enables His people to be creatively and integrally involved in His plan for the redemption of the world. I can think of no truth that is more personally affirming than this. Multitudes of people today are suffering from a poor self-image. This could be cured if we came to appreciate what it means that God Himself has placed us in the body by sovereign choice (1 Cor. 12:18). You are important to God's work of world reconciliation.

2) *The gifts both provide for and necessitate mutual caring.*—We cannot read the account of the early church in the Book of Acts and

not feel an intense longing to belong to a church like that. They experienced such caring fellowship that they could be described as a no-need church. When anyone in the community had a need, those who had a surplus responded by meeting the need. The diaconate ministry in Acts 6 evolved from the concern to minister to the needs of the widows. To meet this pressing need, God granted a new area of gifted ministry. Spiritual gifts enable the church to respond to the needs of the members of the local body of believers. Churches of the nineties are going to be called upon to provide for the total needs of their members. The good news is that God will provide the gift mix necessary to accomplish that ministry task.

We are not to stand alone against the Adversary, we are to stand with the whole army of God.

3) *The gifts promote unity in our diversity.*—The fact that no one can possess all the gifts suggests that there must be a diversity of gifts for the body to function properly. The gifts enable us to celebrate our diversity. Yet our diversity of gifts requires unity of purpose and mind if the church is to function to its full capacity. Unity is not an option for the gifted church. For that reason we read that the apostles were of one mind. Paul constantly reminds the churches of the need to preserve the unity of the spirit. Once we understand the church's commission and the role of the gifts in the fulfillment of that commission, then we must be diligent to preserve the unity of the Spirit.

4) *The gifts remind us of our dependence and our interdependence.*—Since they are by definition "gifts of grace," they call us to humility in the conscious awareness that we are totally dependent upon the grace of God. There is only one answer to the question; "What do you have that you did not receive?" (1 Cor. 4:7) Along this same line of thought, we must also acknowledge that the gifts make us interdependent. I depend upon your gifts to complete mine, and I depend upon your gifts to minister to my needs. In Christ we are so much a part of each other that we can be referred to as a family. Being family means that if you are honored, I can rejoice; and if you suffer, then I am moved to mourning. What affects you affects me.

5) *The proper understanding of the gifts eliminates both spiritual arrogance and spiritual inferiority.*—No matter what gift I possess, I am but one functional member of Christ's body. The world may make value judgments concerning the relative importance of one gift over the other, but every part is equally important to the proper functioning of the body. I cannot sulk in my "I'm of no value" mentality because the Bible teaches that I am uniquely gifted by God and placed into the body by His sovereign choice.

6) *The gifts assure us that no task is too great for the church.*— This is certainly an affirming truth for the local church and its members. What sort of ministry needs will the church be required to meet in the next decade? No one knows for sure. Certainly the world is shrinking and every church will have to think in a more global fashion. The world we live in is becoming increasingly secular, and the church will have to look for new methods of presenting the age-old story of the gospel. The church will experience greater need to mobilize those who have gifts in the arts in order to communicate effectively in this decade. Because of the information explosion, the church will require the services of members who have gifts in areas incorporating new technology. The church will almost certainly be called upon to offer more services to its community in the area of social ministries. The increase in average life span, coupled with the increased cost of living, will provide a unique opportunity for the church to minister to and reach older adults. Ministry to disease victims such as those with AIDS will require the church to use its gifted membership creatively.

The church's greatest responsibility in the employment of its gifted membership is to seek the moving of God's Spirit for their community. Just as the Father's activity determined Jesus' work and ministry, so the Father's activity in our midst must determine the direction of our church's ministry. The understanding of this direction will give the church the clearest guide for determining its mission and thus its gift mix.[2] It goes without saying that the church's first priority in the seeking and employing of its gifts must be prayer. I would recommend that every church begin with *PrayerLife: Walking in Fellowship with God*. This material is available from the Sunday School Board of the Southern Baptist Convention.

While the future will be challenging for the church, it also promises unparalleled opportunities. Will we be prepared to meet those challenges? We will if we function with the full awareness of the

Holy Spirit and His gifts to the church. Remember: We are "His body, the fullness of Him who fills all in all" (Eph. 1:23).

To Him be glory in the church and in Christ Jesus for all generations.

Notes

1. For a discussion of the term "elder" see my book: *The Official Rule Book for the New Church Game* (Nashville: Broadman Press, 1990), ch. 12.

2. Every church should study Henry Blackaby's book, *What the Spirit Is Saying to the Churches* (Atlanta: Home Mission Board, 1988).

Epilogue

News Flash: "Queen Restores Exiled Princess" "Queen Begins Ministry to the Homeless"

What would have been the end of the Snow White story if the queen knew what you know now? If the queen had accepted Christ as Savior and had discovered that her true self-image was found in Him and not in a talking mirror? If she had grown to understand that her self-esteem was not based in her physical beauty but her giftedness? If she had found the security to know that she had value without the crown or the beauty title?

Could you imagine the queen putting her precious talking mirror in the attic and finding her affirmation through God's Word and others to whom she had ministered? The impact such a transformation could have is mind-boggling. She already had the power, prestige, and authority to be seen and heard. Perhaps her experience with Snow White would have led her to develop a ministry to the homeless. Who knows, she could start a Sunday School class for blended families. The royal household could have used one. On the more creative side, she could have used her gifts to develop a support group for widowers. After all, she had been responsible for the deaths of several young women.

You're thinking, *This is too far out!* Oh, really? Remember the apostle Paul. He was a loyal Jew and trained Pharisee. He took advantage of his strong Jewish background and his Roman citizenship to become a major player in persecuting the Christians. Although his actions emanated from his fanatical devotion to Judaism, the results were no better than the queen's! Yet, once he met Christ and discovered his true identity in Him he became a great missionary and apostle to the Gentiles. God transformed Paul's natural leadership abilities into useful spiritual gifts and used him to found a great number of churches. And his was no fairy tale! Walt Disney himself could not have topped that story line.

And it continues to happen today. Drug dealers, prostitutes, crooked officials, famous sports stars, singles, housewives—God can take anyone and give them new life and gift them for service. Perhaps you have always felt left out and insignificant. Maybe the talking mirrors on which you have relied for constant affirmation have let you down. It doesn't have to be that way. God desires to transform you and make you into the image of His Son.

OK, take one more look into the mirror. Will you dare to trust God's word rather than your feelings or the assessment of others? He is your Creator and your Father by spiritual birth. Would He lie to you? Let's look at what He says about you in light of the seven building blocks for strong self-esteem.

• *You Have Inherent Worth.* "He chose you in Him before the foundation of the world" (Eph. 1:4). He adopted you as His child enabling you to call Him, Abba! Father! (Gal. 4:6). You are His heir and fellow heirs with Christ (Eph. 3:6). You have worth to your Father!

• *You Are Secure.* God promises never to leave you or forsake you (Heb. 13:5). Nothing can separate you from the love of God (Rom. 8:39). Your Father will never fail you!

• *You Are Complete.* "You have been made complete" in Christ (Col. 2:10). "The Lord will be your confidence" (Prov. 3:26). Your self-concept is now found in Christ!

• *You Have Purpose.* The Father has commissioned and sent you in the same way He sent Christ (John 20:21). "You are the light of the world" (Matt. 5:14). As a member of the body of Christ, you have an integral role in making God's wisdom known (Eph. 3:10). Your life has purpose both now and for eternity.

• *You Belong.* You belong to the household of God (Eph. 2:19). The Spirit has made you a part of the body of Christ (1 Cor. 12:13). You will never belong to any organization of greater significance than the church.

• *You Are Empowered.* "God is able to make all grace abound to you," enabling you to have a sufficiency for every good work (2 Cor. 9:8). The power that works in you enables you to do exceeding abundantly beyond all you ask or think (Eph. 3:20). You are empowered by God's Holy Spirit.

• *You Are Competent.* "You can do all things through Christ who strengthens" you (Phil. 4:13). Your adequacy depends on the Father and not yourself (2 Cor. 3:6). You have been gifted to serve the Father through the church and He has made you competent.

Perhaps you have always felt left out and insignificant. Maybe the talking mirrors on which you have relied for constant affirmation have let you down. It doesn't have to be that way. God desires to transform you and make you into the image of His Son.

What you see about yourself in God's perfect mirror is a truer and clearer reflection than you will ever receive from another person. Trust God! You are special. You are one of a kind and God made you just the way He wanted you. You may still have rough edges, but God is still working in you to make you like His Son.

As you begin to use your gifts through the body of Christ, you will be affirmed by others who are the recipients of your gifted ministry. When that occurs thank them and thank God. Don't forget to affirm those who minister to you. You can be a good mirror helping others to find their gifted ministry.

God wants you to know that you fit in. Life is not a game or power play or battle of the minds where God teases you by making you wander through life unsure of yourself. Our Father is a loving Father who desires for you to have abundant life. That is precisely the reason He was willing to send His Son to die just for you. Trust God and have faith in Him.

You are a precious member of God's kingdom! If you are OK with your Creator and Heavenly Father, you're OK!

And that's no fairy tale!

What you see about yourself in God's perfect mirror is a truer and clearer reflection than you will ever receive from another person. Trust God! You are special. You are one of a kind and God made you just the way He wanted you.

Appendix A

The ABC's of Salvation*

Some people think a personal relationship with God is something only theologians can comprehend. Actually, God's plan of salvation is simple enough for everyone to understand.

Here are the ABC's of salvation.

A. All persons need salvation. Each of us has a problem the Bible calls sin. Sin is a refusal to acknowledge God's authority over our lives. Everyone who does not live a life of perfect obedience to the Lord is guilty of sin. Since none of us is perfect, all of us are sinners (Rom. 3:10-18).

The result of sin is spiritual death (Ezek. 18:4b). Spiritual death means eternal separation from God. By God's perfect standard we are guilty of sin and therefore subject to the punishment for sin, which is separation from God.

B. God loves each of us. God offers us salvation. Although we have done nothing to deserve His love and salvation, God wants to save us. In the death of Jesus on the cross, God provided salvation for all who would repent of their sins and place their faith in Jesus.

C. Come to Jesus for eternal salvation. The desire in your heart to be saved is the Holy Spirit offering you the forgiveness of your sin and the gift of eternal life. Admit your sin and ask Jesus to deliver you from the consequences of sin. Yield control of your life to Him as your Lord and Savior, and you will be saved (Rom. 10:9-10). Tell your pastor or a Christian friend about your decision.

---

*Originally printed in *Adult Bible Teacher,* April, May, June, 1991 inside cover.

Appendix B

Resources

Discipleship Training Spiritual Gifts Inventory—This is an easy-to-score inventory that tests for the ministry gifts. The "sign" gifts are excluded. This is good for use in a small-group setting. This inventory is available from the Discipleship Training Department of the Baptist Sunday School Board and can be obtained by writing: Material Services, The Baptist Sunday School Board, 127 Ninth Avenue, North, Nashville, Tennessee 37234.

Team Ministry—This gifts inventory tests for functional gifts. The "sign" gifts are excluded. The team ministry inventory shows the intensity level of each gift also. This instrument is available through the Church Growth Institute and can be obtained by writing to them at P. O. Box 4404, Lynchburg, Virginia 24502.

The Spiritual Gifts Inventory—This inventory scores all nineteen gifts listed in the New Testament. Individuals use an answer sheet and then mail the sheet to Growth Points. A personal profile related to giftedness, containing fourteen pages of interpretation, is mailed back to the individual concerning his or her four highest scored gifts. This instrument is available through Growth Points, 4221 Pleasant Valley Road, Suite 125-172, Virginia Beach, Virginia 23464.

The Spiritual Gifts Analysis—Same as above except that it scores only for nine ministry gifts.